OPEN HEART SURGERY

OPEN HEART SURGERY

A Guidebook for Patients and Families

Ina L. Yalof

Introduction by Victor Parsonnet, M.D.
Illustrations by Paul Goldstein

RANDOM HOUSE  NEW YORK

*Grateful acknowledgment is made to the following for permission
to reprint previously published material:*

Harper & Row, Publishers, Inc.: Excerpts from *The Body Has a Head* by
Gustav Eckstein. Copyright © 1969, 1970 by Gustav Eckstein. Reprinted by
permission of Harper & Row, Publishers, Inc.

Random House, Inc.: Excerpt from *Selected Poems* by Stephen Spender.
Copyright 1934 by Stephen Spender; renewed 1962 by Stephen Spender.
Reprinted by permission of the publisher.

Library of Congress Cataloging in Publication Data

Yalof, Ina L., 1939–
Open heart surgery.

Bibliography: p.
Includes index.
1. Heart—Surgery. I. Title.
RD598.Y34   1983   617'.412   82–20537
ISBN 0-394-71513-6

Manufactured in the United States of America

9 8 7 6

For Herbie, with love

Long back, when each of us was a child, in some stillness, some dark night it may have been, he discovered this thing that beats in his chest, this fact. It would be years, if ever, before he could think such a thought as that this was just a muscle contracting. He put his hand there . . . The engine was in him . . .

—GUSTAV ECKSTEIN, *The Body Has a Head*

Introduction

This book is a synopsis of the basics of operable heart disease, directed toward the prospective patient and his family. In order to be effective such a book must be written by a person with extensive firsthand knowledge of patients who have been through the various actual and anticipated consequences of open heart surgery.

Ina Yalof, a medical sociologist, has worked for the past eight years with people who have experienced the benefits and the trials of surgery. As a result of many hours of conversation and personal observation, she can empathize with "her" patients and their families and can speak with some authority about their anxieties and concerns. In acting so often as the doctors' agent she has also come to understand the role they play and how their viewpoints are best presented to the patient. My associates and I are more than grateful to her for the many times she has smoothed the way for us.

The layman's understanding of anatomy and physiology is sometimes so sketchy, even among the relatively well-educated, that meaningful communication between the physician and his patient is difficult. Many people tend not to know the difference between arteries and veins, or what is meant by a heart attack, or, for that matter, where the heart and other organs really lie and what they do. There was a famous English study in which college graduates were asked to draw their idea of the positions of various organs on an outline of the body. The heart was often shown far on the left side of the chest, the lungs were two small circles below the collarbone, and the kidneys were located in the lower abdomen or even in the scrotum. Breaking this type of information barrier is essential in transmitting to the patient the concept of an aortocoronary bypass, a mitral valve replacement, or congestive heart failure.

I have found that the prospect of heart surgery, unlike any other operation, has a special emotional impact, sometimes beyond the rational; perhaps this is because there is a certain mystical association between the heart and life itself. In our daily language we talk frankly and sincerely to one another heart-to-heart. We have heartache for the plight of others, and an especially moving situation touches our hearts. Although our thought processes take place in our brains, we feel with our hearts, the very organ that now requires an operation.

The objective of preoperative education is not simply to inform but to override or allay the patient's spoken and unspoken anxieties and concerns. We must describe the essential features of the disease in understandable terms, not so that the patient will be a medical expert but so that he will comprehend why surgery is the recommended therapy, or at least so that he can compare the benefits of surgical and nonsurgical management of his disease.

A step-by-step description of the hospitalization can also alleviate anxieties so that the patient will not worry about the preoperative tests, and will know something about the environment in the operating room and the recovery areas in advance of the experience. We have learned that proper preoperative education minimizes excessive and unreasoned apprehension, and permits the patient to approach surgery realistically.

Having spent years with open heart patients, Mrs. Yalof has the knowledge and experience to explain the material to the reader clearly and succinctly. All aspects of operable heart disease are presented and indexed. Of special assistance are the descriptive diagrams and illustrations, which make the medical terms more comprehensible.

This book is a source of information and psychological support and, in contrast to that formal document known as "informed consent," reassures the patient by educating him. While it is true that a little knowledge is a dangerous thing, the patient and the patient's family who read this book will find that more than a little knowledge, properly directed and presented, is reassuring and therapeutic.

VICTOR PARSONNET, M.D.

Director of Surgery
Newark Beth Israel Medical Center
Newark, New Jersey

Preface

Wherever the art of medicine is loved,
there also is love of humanity.

—HIPPOCRATES

Open heart surgery, in the chronological sense, is in its late adolescent years. And, as with most teenagers, its growth has been phenomenal. While in the early 1960s open heart surgery was virtually unheard of, in 1981 in the United States alone more than 200,000 people had this operation. Today in medical communities all over the world, its success is heralded with enthusiasm based on a single fact: It works.

The risks and benefits of the operation have probably been discussed with you by your physician. But even the most intelligent person has a difficult time understanding what the specifics of the phrase "you need heart surgery" really are. The medical terminology used to explain the procedure can be confusing to the best of us, and to date there are no blueprints that clearly detail the complexities of the total experience.

As a medical sociologist in contact with cardiac patients, I am concerned that so many people come into the hospital with frighteningly little knowledge about their heart disease. I also think there are far too many misconceptions about the operation. For example, it is widely believed that "open heart surgery" means the heart is cut open. While this is true sometimes, it is not true in most cases. That is because the most common type of open heart surgery is the coronary artery bypass, and in this procedure all repairs are done on the *surface* of the heart. The heart itself is never "opened." What the term actually refers to is the use of a heart-lung machine during a portion of the operation. Whenever this machine takes over the function of the heart and lungs, the patient is said to be having "open heart surgery." It is as simple as that.

But how would a *layman* know this?

. . . just one of the many questions I had in mind when I decided to write this book. Its purpose is to present an informative and comprehensive overview of the surgical experience in words that you can understand. The book describes how the heart works and some of the causes of heart disease. It addresses such relevant matters as selecting a surgeon and paying the bill. And it prepares you for what to expect in the catheterization laboratory, the operating room, the coronary care unit, and when you return home to a life of normal activity.

In short, the book is an "owner's manual" for the prospective heart surgery patient. It is meant not to simplify but to help explain the journey you and your heart are about to undertake. It should be understood that I have in no way intended this book to replace the words of your physician. Rather, the book is designed to be used as an *additional resource* to help you more clearly understand what your doctor is saying.

The information is presented in a generalized manner, as a representation of what "usually" happens. Your cardiologist, your surgeon, or your hospital may vary from the course I describe here. And since no two people respond to surgery in exactly the same fashion, the way I have detailed the duration both of the operation and of the recovery period should also be regarded with flexibility.

To sum up: I have traced the steps a patient takes as he ventures through the experience of open heart surgery. I have attempted to answer some questions; perhaps I have even raised a few. I hope my words will make your journey just a little bit easier. If they do, then my goal in writing this book will have been realized.

I.L.Y.

Acknowledgments

I wish to express my gratitude and respect to Victor Parsonnet, M.D., Director of Surgery at Newark Beth Israel Medical Center, whose friendship I value and to whose teaching I attribute much of whatever good this book will do.

My appreciation to Tobe Alpert; to Drs. Mark S. Hochberg, Ira Pores, S. Mansoor Hussain, Ronald M. Abel, Isaac Gielchinsky, and Daniel Hain; to Erica Eckhardt, R.N., Lester Permut, and Susan Kogan, for the kindness with which they devoted their valuable time to assisting me in this effort; to the American Heart Association, the National Heart, Lung and Blood Institute and the American College of Surgeons for allowing me the unlimited use of their well-researched information; and to Ruth Harrison, Mary Sibiga, Hazel Currie, and Ina Ellen Leeds for their help in the preparation of this manuscript. Finally, I am greatly indebted to the heart surgery team and the heart patients at the Newark Beth Israel Medical Center. Without their generous help, this book could never have been written.

Author's Note

You may notice that throughout this book I have used the word "he" when referring to the patient and the doctor and "she" when referring to the nurse. I did this for no reason other than that I personally find it difficult to read even short articles that use "he/she" every time the singular pronoun is required, and I felt the book would be more readable this way. I sincerely hope no one is offended.

Contents

APPENDICES

OPEN HEART SURGERY

Chapter One

The Development of Heart Surgery: A Brief Look Back

Considering that every time you turn around someone you know is having heart surgery, it's hard to imagine there was ever a time when this operation did not exist.

—RALPH C., fifty-six years old

> I think continually of those who were truly great—the names of those who in their lives fought for life, who wore at their hearts the fire's center.
>
> —STEPHEN SPENDER

LATE ONE SUMMER AFTERNOON in 1897 an Austrian laborer was accidentally stabbed in the heart. At the time it was thought he would never live to see the next sunrise. In a valiant attempt to save the man's life, Ludwig Rehn, a German surgeon, was called upon to open his chest and repair the wound. The success of the operation became a celebrated and much documented "medical miracle," as it was the first time stitches had ever been placed in the human heart.

To describe in any detail what followed, or to acknowledge with any accuracy all those who contributed to events leading up to today's medical miracles, would surely take volumes. Here then are just some of the pioneers whose brilliant efforts in the early days of cardiac surgery led to the development of the field as we now know it.

The year 1939 heralded the beginning of the modern era of heart surgery as surgeons began their attack on congenital heart defects—abnormalities that are present at birth but may not cause problems until later in life. In that year, Dr. Robert Gross, a young surgeon at Boston Children's Hospital, successfully closed a patent ductus arteriosus (an abnormal connection in the blood vessels just above the heart) and thereby transformed a very sick little girl to one in a state of perfect physical health. Shortly thereafter Drs. Gross, Clarence Crafoord, and Alfred Blalock opened new routes to the treatment of other congenital defects when each surgically corrected a significant number of aortic coarctations (a narrowing in the aorta just above the heart). While both of these defects ultimately cause problems with the heart, neither repair directly involved the heart itself.

A major turning point in the surgical management of cardiovascular problems came in 1942, when Drs. Dwight Harken and Charles Bailey and Lord Brock performed a series of mitral commissurotomies, operations used to open up a partially closed heart valve, thereby enabling blood to flow more freely through it. In this early procedure, the surgeon made a small incision into the wall of the beating heart and eased his finger through the mitral valve to gently open the tight valve leaflets. Having easily withstood this invasive surgery, the heart was no longer regarded as "fragile," but was recognized instead as the powerful muscle it actually is.

By the middle of World War II, Dr. Harken was routinely opening chests and removing bullets and shrapnel embedded in the hearts of wounded soldiers—an extraordinary feat in view of the fact that these procedures were performed in makeshift battlefield hospitals. Soon surgeons from all over the world began reporting large numbers of reparative heart operations with successful results in most cases.

Probably the greatest event in the development of cardiac surgery occurred in 1953. Until that time, all operations on the heart had been performed while the heart was still beating. This meant that the surgeon had to operate quickly and was limited in what he could see. In order to repair a more complex heart defect, the heart would have to be stopped, and its function taken over temporarily by a machine. This machine, known as the heart-lung machine, was invented by Dr. John Gibbon, who first used it in that year when he closed a large hole between the two upper heart chambers in an eighteen-year-old girl.

The invention of the heart-lung machine introduced an exciting period in the growth of heart surgery in two main areas: the repair of structural heart defects in children, and the replacement of heart valves in adults. The first two centers to use this machine routinely were located within ninety miles of each other in the state of Minnesota. Dr. C. Walton Lillehei at the University of Minnesota and Dr. John Kirklin at the Mayo Clinic used the heart-lung machine on large numbers of pediatric patients with congenital defects of their hearts.

At about the same time, the development of the artificial heart valve was taken up by Drs. Harken, Albert Starr, and Charles Hufnagel. The idea was to use this valve in cases where an individual's own valve could not be repaired. The first recorded artificial valve replacement took place in 1958. Although the patient did amazingly well, this early success was not immediately followed by continuing good results. In fact, during the first days of heart valve implantations, many patients who received these valves did not survive. Yet the surgeons continued to operate, steadily refining their techniques and improving their equipment. Eventually, an increasing number of patients left the hospital in a renewed state of health and went on to lead normal lives. Word spread quickly throughout the medical community and helped attract more surgeons to the rapidly growing field of cardiac surgery. With the outlook now more optimistic, it was not long before cardiac surgical teams began to appear in dozens of hospitals throughout the country.

Currently, the most frequently performed open heart surgery procedure in the United States is the coronary artery bypass graft. As more fully described in later chapters, this procedure is used to alleviate disabling chest pain and other symptoms in people with narrowed or blocked coronary arteries. Although people had long been suffering with coronary artery disease, the exact site of the problem could not be identified until there were more precise diagnostic tools —specifically, ones that allowed an x-ray view of the coronary arteries.

This project was undertaken by Dr. Werner Forssmann, who performed the first known catheterization of the heart chambers in 1929. At the time, he was thought to be a madman for even suggesting that a catheter could be safely threaded up a vein in the arm and into the heart. Not surprisingly, he could find no volunteers for his experimental procedure. And so it became evident he would have to perform it on himself. By inserting a thin rubber tube into his arm and gently pushing it into the right side of his heart, he was able to take blood samples and measure pressures of an area never before explored. This being done several times without consequence, he then injected a radio-opaque dye through the catheter as his assistant took x-rays. The result: the first pictures of the working heart. For this heroic feat and the monumental contribution it made to the field of cardiology, Dr. Forssmann was rewarded twenty-seven years later with the Nobel Prize.

Coronary arteriography, the procedure involving insertion of a catheter and injection of dye into one or more of the coronary arteries to locate obstructions, was not performed routinely until 1960, when Dr. Mason Sones and his staff at the Cleveland Clinic standardized the technique. With the anatomy of these arteries now clearly defined, the first coronary artery bypass operation was quietly waiting in the wings.

The late 1960s marked the beginning of a spectacular new era in heart surgery with the development of the saphenous vein graft technique to restore the heart's blood supply. Many people played an important role in the early stages, but surgeons such as Effler, Favaloro, Johnson, Spencer, Green, and DeBakey will forever be remembered as the forerunners who displayed an awe-inspiring persistence that ultimately shaped the evolution of the operation.

By 1972, a total of 20,000 bypass operations had been

performed throughout the world. By contrast, only a decade later almost 125,000 bypass operations were done in a single year in the United States *alone*. Recently, studies have been done in which large numbers of postoperative coronary bypass patients were observed, some for as many as ten years after surgery. The results show that in more than 85 percent of the patients, chest pain was significantly relieved, if not cured altogether. And, for some, life has been prolonged.

Probably the most controversial operation in the history of cardiac surgery is the heart transplant. The procedure, which was unthinkable a generation ago, is still considered to be a "last resort," limited to people with irreversible heart failure. Candidates for the operation are people in such critical condition that they would probably not live more than three or four months without a "new" heart. The first transplant was performed on December 3, 1967, by a South African surgeon named Christiaan Barnard. The surgery involved removing the diseased heart from a patient and replacing it with the healthy heart from another (clinically dead) human being. Although it is still a subject of dispute, a few large medical centers, most notably Stanford University under the direction of Dr. Norman Shumway, are having remarkable success.

On December 2, 1982, the first permanent artificial heart, the Jarvik-7, was implanted into the chest of Barney Clark, a sixty-one-year-old retired dentist. The heart was for years the dream of Dr. Willem J. Kolff, a Dutchman, who invented the kidney dialysis machine. It was Kolff's belief that if man can grow a heart, he can build one. The dream became tangible when Dr. Robert Jarvik, who was once Dr. Kolff's assistant, designed the workable device that now carries his name. The plastic and aluminum heart is attached to a 375-pound machine that houses three compressors necessary to ensure its functioning; the patient must be tethered to this machine. The first heart was implanted by Dr. William DeVries at the University of Utah.

The miraculous progress that has been made from the days of the first sutures in the heart to the present research on the permanent artificial heart has been exciting for everyone associated with cardiac surgery. At the moment of writing, heart surgery has become so well established it can honestly be said that for someone who may soon be facing the operation, this is clearly the best and the safest time to have it done.

Chapter Two

The Heart

Actually, I never even thought *about my heart until* *something went wrong with it.*

—HAROLD K., sixty years old

> The heart, ready furnished with its proper organs of motion . . . existed before the body. The first to be formed, nature willed that it should afterwards fashion, nourish, preserve, complete the entire animal, as its work and dwelling place: and as the prince in a kingdom . . .
>
> —WILLIAM HARVEY, 1684

A LTHOUGH MANY PEOPLE think of the heart as a delicate and fragile organ, it is actually a strong and vigorous pump made of muscle tissue.

And the way that it works is beautifully simple.

The heart is a hollow, pear-shaped organ about the size of a clenched fist. It lies inside the chest, behind the breastbone, protected by the rib cage. The heart is divided into four chambers, two upper and two lower. Each upper chamber is called an atrium (or auricle). Each lower chamber is called a ventricle. The atria act as reservoirs, receiving blood from the veins. The ventricles are the pumping chambers, each receiving its blood from an atrium. The left ventricle sends blood to all parts of the body except the lungs. The

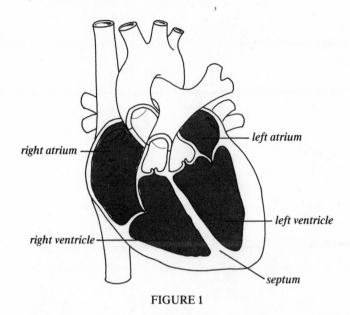

right atrium

left atrium

right ventricle

left ventricle

septum

FIGURE 1

right ventricle, which is thinner-walled than the left, sends blood only to the lungs. The septum, a muscular wall about a half inch thick, separates the right side of the heart from the left side. (Figure 1.)

Four valves in the heart function like one-way doors, allowing blood to flow through them in a single direction. The valves are ringlike structures with two or three tissue flaps, called cusps or leaflets, that open and close depending upon the force of the blood within the heart. The mitral and tricuspid valves are located between the atria and the ventricles, and are known as the atrioventricular (AV) valves or inlet valves. The aortic and pulmonary valves lie between the heart and the aorta and pulmonary artery respectively and are known as the outlet valves because it is through them that blood flows out of the heart.

When the atria fill with blood, the pressure becomes

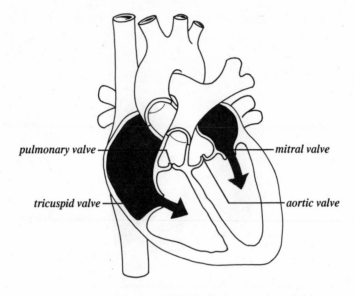

FIGURE 2

higher above the valves than below them. As the atria contract, the pressure of the blood forces the inlet valves open and blood flows freely into the ventricles. (Figure 2.)

When the ventricles become filled with blood, they too contract. As they do, the mitral and tricuspid valves snap shut, preventing blood from flowing backward into the atria. At the same time, the aortic and pulmonary valves open as the blood is forced through them into the aorta and the pulmonary artery respectively. (Figure 3.)

The closing of the valves produces a sound that is interpreted as the "heartbeat" when one listens to the heart with a stethoscope. The sounds are usually described as lub–dub (pause), lub–dub (pause) . . . The first sound is due in part to the closure of the mitral and tricuspid valves, and the second to the closure of the aortic and pulmonary valves.

The circulatory system furnishes life-sustaining food and oxygen to every organ and tissue of the body. These nutrients are carried in the blood and delivered by arteries under pressure (the blood pressure). The circulation process is ongoing as the heart pumps the blood smoothly through the body in a single direction. The trip begins in the lungs, where carbon dioxide is exchanged for oxygen. The bright red (oxygen-rich) blood leaves the lungs through the pulmonary veins, travels to the left atrium, passes through the mitral valve and into the left ventricle. The contraction of the ventricle sends the blood into the aorta, the largest artery in the body. (Figure 4.)

Oxygenated blood flows through the larger arteries into smaller arteries, called arterioles, until it reaches its destination in the capillaries, the tiniest vessels, which link the arteries to the veins. So small are these that the blood cells must line up single-file in order to squeeze through. As they do so, the cells give up oxygen, pick up carbon dioxide and waste products and begin their return trip to the heart. (Figure 5.)

From the smallest veins, the venules, the dark red, oxygen-depleted blood passes into increasingly larger veins until it is finally delivered into the right atrium by the largest veins in the body, the vena cavae. From the right atrium the blood flows into the right ventricle, continues through the pulmonary artery and is brought into the lungs, where carbon dioxide is discharged and oxygen is restored. (Figure 6.)

Like all other muscles in the body, the heart muscle needs its own blood supply for nourishment. Although blood may flow through its chambers, the heart is not fed directly from

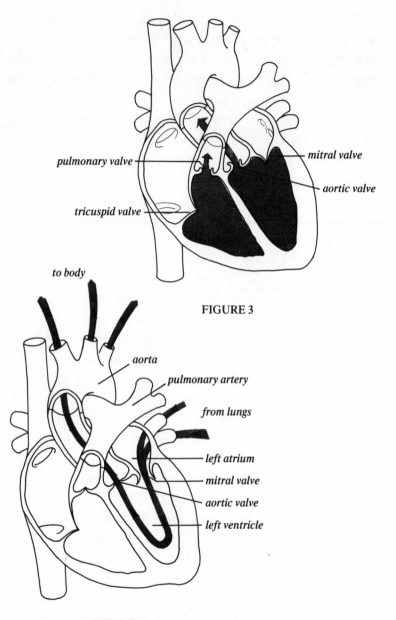

pulmonary valve

tricuspid valve

mitral valve

aortic valve

FIGURE 3

to body

aorta

pulmonary artery

from lungs

left atrium

mitral valve

aortic valve

left ventricle

FIGURE 4

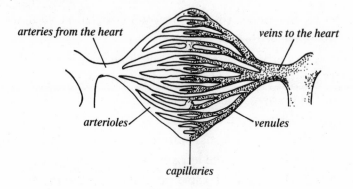

FIGURE 5

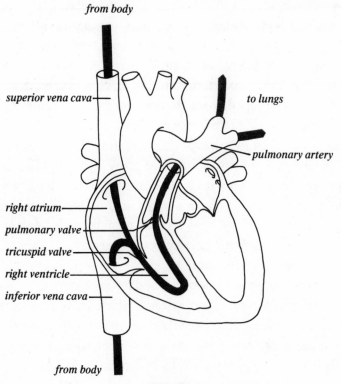

FIGURE 6

there, but rather through its own circulatory system, called the coronary arteries.

The coronary arteries are the first branches of the aorta. They get their name from the Latin word *corona,* which means "crown," because they encircle the heart like a crown. There are two main coronary arteries, the left and the right. The left main coronary artery branches into two slightly narrower arteries: the left anterior descending, which travels down the front of the heart, and the circumflex, which circles around to the back of the heart. These bring the major blood supply to the heart's left side. The right coronary artery delivers blood to the right side of the heart. Only 1/4 inch wide at their widest, the coronary arteries divide into progressively smaller branches as they wind their way down the heart, farther and farther from the aorta. Because of their location the coronary arteries are the first to receive fresh blood as it is pumped from the left ventricle. (Figure 7.)

Sometimes if a large coronary artery becomes narrowed, as can happen from coronary artery disease, the smaller arteries farther downstream begin to grow wider and longer and eventually join up with small branches of another artery in an attempt to compensate for the loss of blood supply. This natural process of new arterial growth and development is called collateral circulation (Figure 8).

The mechanical function of the heart—pumping the blood on its route throughout the body—is governed by the heart's electrical conduction system. Electrical signals and currents within the heart regulate its rhythm, that is, the contracting motions of the atria and ventricles. The tiny signals begin in a group of cells called the sinoatrial (SA) node, located at the top of the right atrium. The SA node

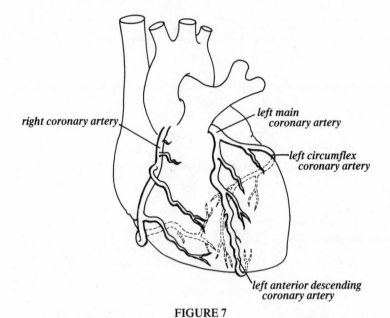

FIGURE 7

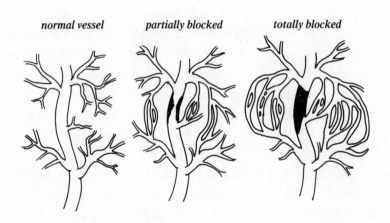

FIGURE 8

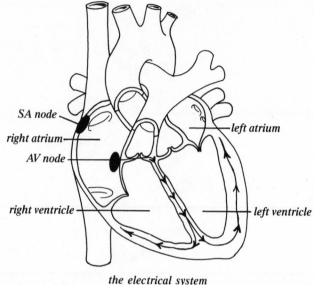

the electrical system
FIGURE 9

sets the pace for the heartbeat. From there the electrical current radiates throughout the heart, starting at its origin in the right atrium and following a pathway of special muscle fibers to the atrioventricular (AV) node in the center of the heart. These fibers can be thought of as tissue wires through which electrical signals are conducted at a speed of 16 feet per second. The current passes from the atria to the ventricles, which, in turn, contract. It is by this process that the heart contracts and relaxes in a rhythmic pattern, at a normal rate of 60 to 80 beats per minute. (Figure 9.)

The circulatory system within the body consists of 60,000 miles of blood vessels. These, laid end to end, would circle the world nearly three times. Yet only ten pints of blood flow within them. The heart beats an average of 100,000 times a day, each beat lasting but a fraction of a single second. With each beat, 2 1/2 ounces of blood are sent to the body—1,000 gallons every twenty-four hours. The heart can circulate the entire body's blood supply once each minute while a person is resting, four times that when he climbs two flights of stairs. With proper care, a healthy heart should continue its work, without missing a beat, for an average of seventy-two years.

Chapter Three

Understanding
Heart Disease

I knew something was wrong inside, but I never thought I'd need surgery *to fix it. I still remember the exact moment when they told us . . . I could hear my heart beating . . . I could hear everyone's heart.*

—SIDNEY H., forty-two years old

> If another doctor had come along with a better explanation, I would have happily seized it.
>
> —HENRY KISSINGER in *People Weekly,* April 5, 1982, talking about his heart surgery

MANY DISORDERS can affect the heart. Among them are high blood pressure, rheumatic heart disease, narrowed coronary arteries, congenital defects, and abnormal heart rhythms. The unfortunate statistic is that cardiovascular disease claims the lives of nearly one million Americans each year—making it the nation's number one killer and the probable cause of more deaths than all other diseases combined.

The mechanism of heart disease, namely, how and why it happens, is perhaps easier to understand if we liken the heart to a mechanical pump. Blood comes into the heart like liquid into a pump, and leaves it at a regulated rate. Like all machines, the heart needs energy to function, and, as with all machines, things can go wrong. Sometimes a particular part of the heart does not work correctly from birth, and at other times, after functioning well for a number of years, things may begin to break down. Although almost any part of the heart can become defective, the most common problems occur in the vessels that deliver blood to the heart muscle or in the valves that regulate the direction of the flow of blood through the heart chambers. The electrical conduction system of the heart can also malfunction; or there may be disease in the heart muscle itself.

Heart disease may be congenital, meaning the defect is present at birth, or it may be acquired, beginning later in life. Congenital disease is becoming less common, perhaps due to better prenatal care, while acquired diseases of the heart and blood vessels continue to be a major health problem.

CORONARY ARTERY DISEASE

Coronary artery disease is by far the most common form of cardiac disorder in this country, involving five million people and causing as many as 1.5 million heart attacks each year. Although a variety of diseases may affect the coronary arteries, in 99 percent of the cases the problem is atherosclerosis. This term is often confused with arteriosclerosis, which is a general term meaning "hardening of the arteries." Atherosclerosis is a specific kind of arteriosclerosis in which the inner layer of the artery wall becomes thickened by soft fatty deposits called atheromas. Any of the arteries in the body can be involved, but the ones most commonly and

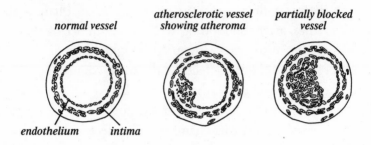

normal vessel

atherosclerotic vessel
showing atheroma

partially blocked
vessel

endothelium   intima

FIGURE 10

seriously affected are the arteries leading to the heart, brain, kidneys, and legs.

The disease process begins with a tiny break in the endothelium, the thin layer of cells that coats the inside of the artery and protects the next layer, the intima. For some unknown reason, and at any time, the endothelium may allow a small amount of fat (lipid) to become deposited beneath it. In time, more fats and other materials carried in the bloodstream gather around this deposit, forming a fibrous plaque. As the plaque increases in size it subsequently decreases the internal diameter of the vessel and thereby restricts the flow of blood (Figure 10).

The exact cause of atherosclerosis still is not known. What *is* known is that plaques begin to appear in the arteries early in life and progress at a rate that varies from person to person. It has also been suggested, after many years of scientific research, that a group of factors, individually or in combination, may play an important part in the premature development or rapid progression of the disease. These risk factors, which include smoking, high blood pressure, high cholesterol, and diabetes, will be discussed in detail in the next chapter.

ANGINA

When a coronary artery is narrowed, the blood supply to the heart muscle is diminished, causing a condition called ischemia, inadequate delivery of blood to a muscle. Angina, a symptom of ischemia, is usually described as a dull squeezing or crushing sensation occurring in the middle of the chest and sometimes radiating to the neck, arms, or jaw.

There are various forms of angina; the most common types are stable and unstable. Stable angina is brought on at times when the heart is summoned to increase its pumping activity (as can happen with something as simple as eating a hearty meal or as strenuous as shoveling snow) and therefore needs more oxygen. If the coronary arteries are obstructed and unable to supply the extra blood and oxygen that the heart requires at that time, the heart will complain with the feelings described above. Stable angina characteristically lasts less than twenty minutes and is relieved after the activity that has put increased demands on the heart muscle is discontinued, or after nitroglycerin is taken. Nitroglycerin is a drug that temporarily increases blood supply to the heart by dilating (enlarging) the blood vessels. This type of angina is often predictable, and can continue on and off for months or even years, usually remaining at the same intensity. Sometimes it may disappear if adequate collateral circulation develops.

Unstable angina is a more serious variety in that it is often difficult to relieve. It can occur with minimal or no exertion, as well as with effort or stress. Its onset is often unpredictable, and it is not always relieved by rest. Unstable angina may be a warning of an impending heart attack, although it is possible to have unstable angina and never have a heart attack.

A third type of angina, called atypical or variant angina, often happens during rest or sleep. This type of angina is thought to be related to coronary spasm, which is discussed in detail later in this chapter.

HEART ATTACK

The medical term for a heart attack is myocardial infarction. This usually results when one or more of the coronary artery branches are severely narrowed by an enlarging plaque and become sealed off by a blood clot (thrombus) forming on the plaque or lodging in the narrowed area of the vessel. The process, called coronary thrombosis, abruptly interrupts blood flow to the portion of the heart muscle supplied by the affected artery. When heart muscle tissue is deprived of oxygen, which is carried in the blood, it becomes severely damaged or dies. (Figure 11.)

The most common symptom of a heart attack is severe chest pain that is much like angina in quality, but more intense. It is often described as a heavy, crushing, viselike sensation and it is not uncommon to hear a patient say he felt as though an elephant were sitting on his chest. The pain from a heart attack is nearly always centered under the breastbone but may radiate to the left arm and the jaw, the back of the neck, or the shoulder. It is seldom relieved by nitroglycerin or other antianginal drugs. Anxiety, sweating, nausea and vomiting, shortness of breath, and fainting can all be symptoms of a heart attack and may occur alone or in combination.

A heart attack can be massive, or it may be so mild that occasionally a person will find that he has had an old infarction of which he was never aware. This happens when the pain was so minimal that the symptoms were ignored, or the duration of symptoms was so short that the victim attributed it to a familiar discomfort such as indigestion and quickly dismissed it.

The severity of a heart attack depends chiefly on the area of the heart that is involved and the amount of muscle that

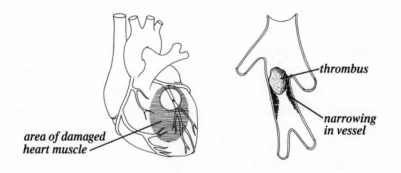

coronary thrombosis
FIGURE 11

has been damaged. If a heart attack interferes with the electrical pathways of the heart, it can lead to dangerously abnormal heart rhythms (arrhythmias), such as ventricular fibrillation. When this happens all the fibers of the ventricle quiver independently rather than contracting in a coordinated way, and the blood remains in the ventricle rather than being pumped throughout the body. In effect, the heart has stopped beating, and blood stops circulating. A fibrillating heart can often be reverted to normal by a strong electrical stimulus from a device known as a defibrillator. Unfortunately, such equipment is available only in hospitals or ambulances. To save the patient's life, defibrillation must be accomplished within a few minutes. In the absence of a defibrillator, the circulation may be artificially maintained for a while by a technique called cardiopulmonary resuscitation (CPR) until defibrillation can be performed.

A mild heart attack results in damage to a small amount of heart muscle. When the damaged area heals there may be no impairment of heart function. But if the attack destroys a larger area, the consequences can be more severe. For example, when a large portion of muscle is lost, there may not be enough healthy muscle left for the heart to function properly. At this point, the patient is said to be in heart failure.

HEART FAILURE

The term *failure* has a ring of finality to it that is generally misleading. In fact, people with chronic heart failure may do well for many years, especially if they are treated with the appropriate medicines. What heart failure actually means is that the heart muscle is unable to pump sufficient blood to maintain adequate circulation, especially under conditions of any increased demand. Congestive heart failure can be a chronic condition that causes fluid retention in various parts of the body. It may develop slowly over a period of years as a result of a combination of a number of different conditions, such as high blood pressure, valvular defects, and, most commonly, heart muscle damage resulting from one or more heart attacks. When the heart does not empty properly, blood returning to it through the major veins backs up and collects in the veins of the lungs, ankles, and legs, causing swelling or edema. The symptoms produced are shortness of breath, an inability to sleep except in a semisitting position, and overall fatigue. It is for this condition that drugs to enhance urine flow (diuretics) and to strengthen heart muscle contraction (digitalis) are used.

Acute heart failure is usually caused by massive, irreversible heart muscle damage from a severe heart attack. In its most serious form, it may lead to collapse of the entire circulatory system, a situation known as cardiogenic shock, which carries an extremely poor outlook.

VENTRICULAR ANEURYSM

An aneurysm of the left ventricle is a common complication that may result from a heart attack. After an attack the damaged heart tissue sometimes becomes weak and thin and begins to balloon out, creating a saclike area in the wall of the heart that contracts barely, if at all. This area of bulging and functionless muscle greatly decreases the efficiency of the heart's pumping action. Blood tends to pool in an aneurysm, and may form a clot within the chamber of the ventricle, further increasing the work load of the heart and reducing its output of blood. (Figure 12.)

CORONARY SPASM

Coronary spasm, although often occurring in conjunction with coronary heart disease, is a distinctly separate entity that also may produce angina and heart attacks. Spasm is a sudden, temporary contraction of a segment of an artery, diseased or not, lasting long enough to impede the flow of blood to the heart, yet often leaving no trace of ever having occurred. The result may be identical to an arteriosclerotic blockage—little or no blood can flow through the vessel in spasm, therefore little or no oxygen reaches the heart muscle. Consequently, chest pain or a heart attack can result. Nitroglycerin is effective in relieving the spasm and permitting increased flow through the vessels. And several new drugs now on the market, such as nifedipine and verapamil, are extremely effective in preventing spasm.

VALVULAR DISEASE

A diseased or defective valve interferes with the normal one-way flow of blood as it is pumped through the heart. To compensate for a poorly functioning valve, the heart must pump harder. Eventually, the effects of overwork are felt in the symptoms of valvular disease.

Although there are four valves in the heart, valvular disease generally involves the two valves on the left side, the mitral and aortic valves. Perhaps this is because the left ventricle, the major pumping chamber, has a pressure five times greater than the right ventricle. Heart valves may be defective at birth or they may be damaged by disease later in life.

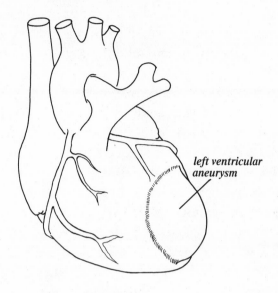

left ventricular
aneurysm

FIGURE 12

The most common type of valve disease is rheumatic heart disease, which results from rheumatic fever. Rheumatic fever, which does not affect the heart directly, is a secondary reaction to certain infections that can occur with "strep throat." In some cases the infection produces scarring of the valves and weakens the heart muscle. Although rheumatic fever most often strikes children between the ages of five and fifteen, the symptoms of the damage left in its wake may not become apparent until much later. Frequently rheumatic fever is so mild that it is never even diagnosed.

Rheumatic heart disease attacks the mitral valve more often than any of the other valves, causing inflammation at first. During the healing process scar tissue may cause portions of the affected leaflets to partially fuse together, producing a buttonhole appearance. The valve leaflets do not lose their mechanical function immediately, but become slightly rigid and gradually degenerate as the patient gets older. As the leaflets become more rigid, the heart becomes burdened and symptoms of mitral valve disease start to appear.

Another cause of valve malfunction is the natural aging process that most commonly affects the aortic valve. As can occur with other structures in the body, calcium carried in the blood can build up on a heart valve, thereby decreasing the flexibility of its leaflets.

A normal heart valve is flexible enough to open and permit blood to flow through it, yet strong enough to hold back the flow when closed. A diseased valve may be affected in two ways: it may be too tight to open all the way, hindering forward blood flow, or it may be too loose to close completely, permitting backward flow. The former is termed stenotic, which means "tight," and the latter is called insufficient, which describes valve leaflets that are too loose or are leaking.

The symptoms of a stenotic valve vary depending on which valve is affected. If the mitral valve is stenotic, it retards the free flow of blood from the left atrium to the left ventricle. When this happens, blood that is returning from the lungs to the left atrium backs up, causing the lungs to fill up with fluid, a condition known as pulmonary congestion. The advanced form of pulmonary congestion is pulmonary edema, in which fluid accumulates both in the lungs and in the space around the lungs.

Symptoms caused by pulmonary congestion begin as shortness of breath upon exertion. This gradually increases to shortness of breath while resting. Eventually, as the air sacs in the lungs become increasingly filled with fluid, the person may awaken during the night with severe difficulty in breathing and may be forced to sleep in a sitting position.

If the aortic valve has become stenotic, the normal amount of blood from the left ventricle cannot be pumped easily into the aorta. This may result in an insufficient amount of blood being delivered to the vital organs of the body, including the brain and the heart itself. The symptoms produced are lightheadedness and fatigue. Longstanding stenosis imposes an excessive strain on the heart muscle, which may begin to weaken or fail, further aggravating the condition.

Aortic stenosis may also be congenital. It may be due to a narrowed aortic valve, to a buildup of extra tissue just above the aortic valve, or to buildup of muscle tissue on the left ventricle just below the aortic valve. Congenital aortic stenosis may not become apparent until the valve becomes so obstructed that the adult patient develops symptoms of left ventricular failure.

The second most common valve problem is insufficiency, in which the valve leaflets are either too flexible, sometimes even floppy, or so stiff that they cannot close completely. If the mitral valve is insufficient, some of the blood in the left ventricle flows backward into the left atrium and must be pumped out again. Similarly, in aortic insufficiency some of the blood in the aorta leaks back into the ventricle when the ventricle relaxes. The backward flow through valves that no longer close tightly produces a sound known as a heart murmur. This backward movement of blood is called regurgitation.

Sometimes a valve does not function properly as a result of an infection called bacterial endocarditis. Any infection in the body may release bacteria into the bloodstream. They can lodge on the valve, creating a new site of infection. When this occurs, the bacteria from the valves are repeatedly released into the bloodstream, causing bacteremia. If unchecked or untreated, the infection on the valves can lead to loss of valve function and severe problems related to valvular insufficiency.

CONGENITAL HEART DEFECTS

A congenital heart defect is one that develops in the fetal heart or in a major blood vessel near the fetal heart. According to the *American Heart Association Fact Book,* approximately eight out of every 1,000 children born in the United States have congenital heart disease; for some reason the heart of the fetus has not developed properly. In most instances it is not known why this occurs, but there is strong evidence that German measles may be one cause. If a woman contracts German measles during the first three months of pregnancy, the disease may interfere with the development of the baby's heart. Infections and genetic errors are other causes of congenital heart defects.

Septal Defects

The most common congenital defect is an abnormal opening (actually a small hole) in the septum, the muscular wall that divides the left and right sides of the heart. The problem may be an atrial septal defect (ASD), in which case the opening is between the two atria, or it may be a ventricular septal defect (VSD), where the opening is between the two ventricles. As a result of these defects, blood is shunted between the two atria or the two ventricles (Figure 13).

Since the pressure is ordinarily greater on the left side of the heart, the blood usually is forced from the left to the right side, from where it is pumped to the lungs. But if the pressure on the right side is high, as is the case when there is an obstruction in the pulmonary artery, oxygen-poor blood is forced from the right side to the left side before it has had a chance to pick up oxygen in the lungs. The oxygen-poor blood then circulates through the aorta to the rest of the body, creating a blue cast to the skin. Infants with this problem are sometimes called "blue babies." Some septal defects are so small that they produce no symptoms and may require no treatment. They may even close spontaneously as the child gets older. The larger ones usually require surgical correction, however.

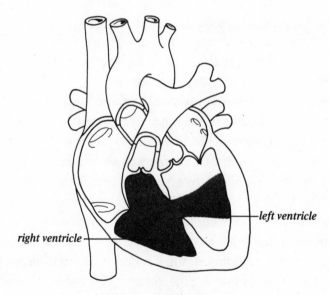

ventricular septal defect

FIGURE 13

Patent Ductus Arteriosus

Another common defect is a patent ductus arteriosus (PDA). In the unborn baby, there is a vessel (ductus) connecting the pulmonary artery and the aorta. This vessel usually closes itself off twenty-four to forty-eight hours after birth. When it fails to close, the baby's blood is shunted from the aorta to the pulmonary artery and then to the lungs. This allows some of the oxygenated blood to be delivered to the lungs. The symptoms of this defect are early fatigue and, at times, slow physical growth. The vessel can sometimes be encouraged to close by the administration of certain drugs, or a closed heart surgical procedure can be performed to close off the ductus. (Figure 14.)

Coarctation of the Aorta

Coarctation of the aorta is a severe narrowing of the aortic arch, causing it to resemble an hourglass (Figure 15). The pinched segment partially obstructs the flow of blood through the aorta to the lower half of the body. The result is high blood pressure in the upper arms, head, and neck and low blood pressure in the lower body.

Surgical correction of a coarctation should be performed when the child is about five years of age. This allows the vessel to become large enough for the surgeon to repair easily and is still early enough to avoid complications from the longstanding high blood pressure. If surgery is not performed in early childhood, small blood vessels will begin to grow above and below the narrowing. This collateral circulation system may be sufficient to postpone symptoms until later childhood or early adolescence.

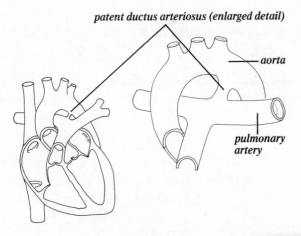

patent ductus arteriosus (enlarged detail)

aorta

pulmonary artery

patent ductus arteriosus

FIGURE 14

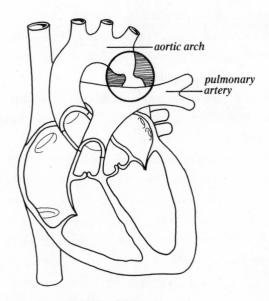

aortic arch

pulmonary artery

coarctation of the aorta

FIGURE 15

PROBLEMS OF THE ELECTRICAL CONDUCTION SYSTEM

The normal heart beats rhythmically as a result of the transmission of tiny electrical currents from the sinoatrial node in the right atrium to the atrioventricular node in the center of the heart and ultimately throughout the entire ventricle. The current brings about an electrochemical interaction in the cells that immediately causes the chambers to contract and relax. If the electrical pathways are disrupted, the heart no longer beats rhythmically. An abnormal heart rhythm is called an arrhythmia. The heart may beat too slowly, producing an arrhythmia known as bradycardia (heart rate under 60 beats per minute); it may beat too rapidly, a condition known as tachycardia (heart rate over 100 beats per minute); or it may become erratic.

The most dangerous arrhythmia is ventricular fibrillation, a disorganized quivering of the heart muscle, which, if not treated immediately, can lead to death. But if the person is fortunate enough to be in a place where help is available, the heart may be electrically shocked into normal rhythm in a matter of minutes.

The most common problem of the electrical conduction system is bradycardia. When the heart beats more slowly than normal, insufficient blood is delivered to the body. The effects are felt first in the brain, as lightheadedness, dizziness, fainting spells, blurred vision, or shortness of breath. Tachycardia, on the other hand, sometimes produces a pounding sensation in the chest. It also produces a low cardiac output because the heart contracts too rapidly to allow time for normal filling of the ventricles.

Irregular heart rhythms can be associated with valvular disease, coronary artery disease, or heart attacks. Most often, however, they are simply the result of the normal aging process. With age, some of the conduction fibers in the heart muscle begin to wear out, causing a temporary interruption in the signal relay. Some of these problems are corrected by the implantation of a pacemaker, which delivers artificial electrical impulses that cause the heart to contract. This will be discussed in a later chapter on support systems.

Chapter Four

Risk Factors for Coronary Artery Disease

The doctor mentioned the various risk factors I had and made it quite clear that I would have to take these things into consideration from now on. I suppose if you think about the trade-off, it's really a very small price to pay.

—ABNER B., fifty-one years old

To promise not to do a thing is the surest way in the world to make a body want to go and do that very thing.

—MARK TWAIN, *The Adventures of Tom Sawyer*

RISK FACTORS are those traits, habits, or conditions that are associated with an increased possibility of an individual's developing coronary artery disease, and that are now felt to be directly related to an individual's life style and habits. Considering the overall change in the way of life of millions of Americans over the past fifty years, it is not surprising that the incidence of coronary artery disease has more than doubled in this country in the twentieth century.

For example, years ago most men's jobs required physical labor, while for women housework meant cooking, cleaning, washing by hand, and walking daily to the market. Sundays were spent resting from a physically taxing work week. But now, many people sit at their desks five or six days a week and use their leisure time for physical activities. The automobile and mass transportation have eliminated the need for much walking, and mechanization has eased the most strenuous occupations. Add to this the multitude of stressful situations at work and at home, the availability and promotion of cigarettes, and an elevation in the socioeconomic status of our society that has allowed more people to afford a diet of foods high in fats and cholesterol. Some factors in this portrait would be highly appealing to many less fortunate people around the world. Yet the trade-off seems to be a society in which more than 600,000 people die each year from cardiovascular disease.

What, then, are these risk factors, how are they related to heart disease, and how can they be avoided?

The four factors thought to be the most contributory are smoking, high blood pressure (hypertension), high levels of blood lipids (fatty substances), and diabetes. Other risk factors include a family history of cardiovascular disease, obesity, a sedentary life style, and emotional stress. Studies indicate that when two or more major factors are present simultaneously, the risk is multiplied.

Risk factors are generally classified as uncontrollable, meaning they cannot be changed (age, sex, and heredity), or controllable (high cholesterol levels, hypertension, smoking, diabetes, obesity, sedentary life style, emotional stress, and perhaps personality type). Although most physicians acknowledge the role played by risk factors in the development of atherosclerosis, it is important to mention that there are no direct scientific data to prove that elimination or correction of these factors can reverse or prevent coronary artery disease. Growing evidence, however, does point in this direction.

UNCONTROLLABLE RISK FACTORS
Age
Atherosclerosis is, in part, a condition or disease of aging. Quite simply, the longer a person lives, the greater are his chances of developing the disease. There is evidence that atherosclerosis begins as early as childhood, yet it progresses so slowly that it may not become apparent for many years. Still, researchers hope that with increased knowledge of its causes, they will be able to retard its development before it reaches the advanced stages. There is already strong evidence that the last ten years have seen a distinct reduction in atherosclerosis.

Sex
Statistics show that premenopausal women are less likely to develop coronary artery disease than men. This is thought to be related to natural female sex hormones, which may affect the properties in the blood that cause atherosclerotic plaques to develop in the arteries. This possible explanation is strengthened by the fact that after approximately age sixty, women and men develop the disease at a similar rate. In recent years, however, women have become afflicted earlier and in greater numbers than in the past. Women are now smoking more, have entered the competitive job mar-

ket in greater numbers, and in many ways are subject to the same stress as their male counterparts. As their attitudes and life styles more closely resemble men's, their incidence of coronary artery disease is fast approaching that of men.

Heredity

A genetic tendency toward development of coronary artery disease exists, but to what extent no one is exactly sure. Some researchers believe that people whose parents had the disease are at greater risk before the age of fifty than those whose parents have no history of it. After fifty, however, the tendency to develop coronary artery disease equalizes for the two groups. Understanding of the word *tendency* is key. It means only that the possibility is greater: it should be stressed that not everyone with a family history of coronary artery disease will develop it, and conversely the disease can develop in people with no family history of it. In addition to the possibility of an inherited genetic influence, the home environment may play a role. Children tend to pattern themselves after their parents. Children of obese parents are often prone to obesity themselves, probably because they acquire their parents' eating habits. Similarly, smoking and sedentary life styles may also be the result of childhood observations.

CONTROLLABLE RISK FACTORS

Hypertension

Blood pressure is the result of two factors: the amount of blood pumped from the heart with each beat, and the resistance within the blood vessels as the blood flows through them. Essential hypertension, also known as high blood pressure, is an excessive amount of pressure within the vessel walls. Picture, for example, a garden hose with a flow-regulating nozzle at the far end. If the nozzle is wide open, water from the faucet will flow easily through the hose. If the nozzle is partially closed, water pumped in will expand the hose, the amount of expansion depending on how fast the water can get out through the nozzle. If the hose is rigid, the pressure developing within it will be even higher.

The bloodstream is something like water running through a hose. Blood is pumped from the heart and flows through the arteries into the capillaries. If the smallest arteries (the arterioles) are narrowed at the point where they become capillaries, the result is similar to what happens when the hose nozzle is partially closed: the pressure within the larger arteries will be high, and higher still if the arteries have become stiff or rigid with age. The tighter the narrowing, the higher the pressure and the more damage to the artery walls. Similarly, if more blood is pumped into the arteries (a high blood volume that can occur with excessive salt intake, for example), the pressure will be still higher. As a result, the heart must work harder to circulate the blood against this excessive amount of resistance within the small artery bed.

Average blood pressure is approximately 120/80. When the heart contracts (systole) it exerts 120 mm Hg (millimeters of mercury) pressure on the wall of the artery. When it rests (diastole), the pressure falls to 80 mm Hg. Some people refer to a "normal" blood pressure, but it is important to understand that pressure values vary from person to person, and what is normal for one may not be normal for another. The higher the elevation of the blood pressure, the greater the risk to health. The major risks are heart failure, kidney failure, and stroke.

Several things may be done to help control hypertension. A salt-restricted diet is helpful, since the sodium in salt causes the body to retain fluid; if salt intake and therefore the total volume of fluid in the body are decreased, the heart has less blood to circulate. Diuretics are also used as a method of removing excess fluid. Drugs called vasodilators relax and dilate the blood vessels, thereby reducing resistance in flow against which the heart must pump. Treatment must be under the careful direction of a physician and must be constant and monitored regularly.

Cholesterol

One of the chief suspects in the cause of coronary artery disease is cholesterol, a fatty yellow material that is normally carried in the blood. Cholesterol is manufactured by the liver as part of the process of digestion, and it is also found in many of the foods we eat. Although the body needs a certain amount of cholesterol, an excessive amount can be detrimental, because there is evidence that extra blood cholesterol can build up in the walls of the arteries and may lead to or accelerate the process of atherosclerosis.

Cholesterol and other fats are transported in the bloodstream in soluble form as components of lipoproteins (a complex of fat and protein molecules). The major function of the high-density lipoprotein (HDL) is to remove cholesterol from the cells and deliver it to the liver and other sites where it can be metabolized or eliminated. By keeping the fats contained, HDLs actually appear to protect the artery against atherosclerosis. According to a 1981 study on arteriosclerosis, reported by the National Heart, Lung and Blood Institute, an inverse relationship has been identified between the concentration of HDL cholesterol in the blood and coronary heart disease. In other words, individuals with high levels of HDL tend to have a low risk of coronary heart disease. Conversely, low-density lipoproteins (LDL) are responsible for transporting cholesterol to the cells. This can increase fatty buildup in the arteries and contribute to premature heart disease.

An increasing number of studies shows that blood fats may be lowered through proper diet. Diets high in saturated fats tend to raise the level of blood cholesterol, whereas diets high in polyunsaturated fats tend to lower it. What remains questionable is to what extent the reduction affects the rate of development of coronary artery disease. It is also unclear if lowering cholesterol can be helpful once the symptoms of coronary artery disease have begun. Although many issues are still being debated, one thing does remain clear: reducing cholesterol cannot be harmful and may, in fact, be beneficial.

Cholesterol levels vary in each individual, often depending on age, sex, or even what time of day the blood sample was taken. A cholesterol level of about 210 mg/dl in middle-aged men is considered to be acceptable by most physicians. When the level exceeds that amount, changes in diet and living habits may be suggested. These might include:

—Lowering the overall amount of fat in the diet, since fat increases body weight, and obesity is known to be a contributing factor to coronary artery disease.

—Being selective about the type of fat in the diet by substituting polyunsaturated fats for saturated fats (for more information on this, see the section on diet in Chapter Thirteen).

—Drinking only in moderation. Alcohol has an effect on the way the body metabolizes fats.

—Taking medicines as prescribed. Antilipids are effective at times in lowering cholesterol levels but use of these drugs must be carefully supervised.

Cigarette Smoking

The label of every pack reads: "Warning: The Surgeon General has determined that cigarette smoking is dangerous to your health." The label used to say, ". . . may be detrimental." The change should tell us something. *There is no longer any doubt that cigarette smoking contributes to coronary artery disease.* Nicotine makes the heart beat faster, causes the blood vessels to constrict, and creates turbulence inside the arterial walls, thereby making it easier for cholesterol to enter them. It may also interfere with the liver's ability to dispose of fats carried in the bloodstream, increasing the chance that these fats will collect in the arteries. Additionally, inhaling cigarette smoke increases the carbon monoxide level in the blood, reducing the amount of oxygen the blood can carry to the tissues and requiring the heart to work harder to keep the body supplied.

Everyone seems to be aware that smoking causes lung cancer, but not everyone realizes that the risk of dying from heart disease is three times greater than that of dying from lung cancer. The death rate from a heart attack is 50 to 200 percent higher in heavy cigarette smokers than in nonsmokers. Fortunately, this risk gradually declines to the same level as that of nonsmokers if the habit is given up. Within two weeks of nonsmoking, carbon monoxide levels in the blood are completely reduced to normal. Within two years the risk of a heart attack in former smokers is half that of smokers. Within fifteen years, the risk is the same as for nonsmokers.

An obvious way to avoid the consequences of this risk factor is to *stop smoking,* a feat we all know is easier said than done. Listed in the appendix on patient resources are programs and literature that may be of help to those who need assistance in giving up cigarettes.

Diabetes

Diabetes mellitus is a condition in which the body fails to produce the amount of insulin it requires. Insulin is a hormone manufactured in the pancreas and used by the body to metabolize sugar and other carbohydrates. When an inadequate amount of insulin is produced, sugar accumulates in the blood. Higher levels of blood sugar increase the cholesterol level, to the degree that it may cause early development of atherosclerosis.

The cause of diabetes has not yet been determined. It is thought to be inherited in some people. Those who develop diabetes at an early age have a greater risk of developing atherosclerosis than those in whom the disease occurs in later years. Obese people are more likely to develop diabetes than thin people since their cells are less responsive to the insulin secreted by the pancreas. Fortunately, diabetes may be kept under control with medicine, dietary management, and weight regulation. Although it is not certain that proper management of diabetes results in a decrease in the development of atherosclerosis, evidence suggests that this is true.

Obesity

The medical definition of obesity is "weight of twenty or more pounds above normal." Obesity generally develops from overeating or taking in more calories than are burned in the day's activities. Excess weight does not directly affect the heart itself, but it does intensify other risk factors. For example, part of the connection between obesity and heart disease is due to the fact that obesity increases a person's chance of developing hypertension, an elevated amount of cholesterol in the blood, and diabetes. In fact, diabetes is one of the chief health problems of the obese individual. Obese people are also more likely to have low levels of high-density lipoproteins in their blood. (As was described earlier in this chapter, these are the lipoproteins that help protect against atherosclerosis.) Finally, because it is sometimes difficult for an obese person to move about with ease, quite often the alternative becomes a sedentary life style, which is in itself a risk factor for coronary heart disease.

Weight loss can bring the body chemistry back to normal levels, but dieting should always be done under the supervision of a physician. Suggestions on how to lose weight can be found in the section on weight in Chapter Thirteen.

Sedentary Life Style

There is no question that activity and exercise are essential to maintain a healthy heart and good circulation. Yet over half of the adult population in the United States does little in the way of exercise. In today's society the expanded use of mechanical energy to replace human physical energy has led to increased physical inactivity. Perhaps this is one reason why so many people today have weight problems and cardiovascular diseases.

Exercise strengthens the heart muscle, because exertion requires the heart to pump more blood. A stronger heart pumps out more blood per beat and therefore does not need to beat as often. Exercise also helps reduce stress because it lowers the level of hormones that speed up the heart rate and increase blood pressure. It may also be an aid in losing weight. What is not known scientifically is why *lack* of exercise contributes to the development of coronary artery disease. It has been suggested that those who are not physically active may have higher cholesterol levels and may tend to be overweight.

A regular program of sustained exercise generally has positive effects on physical fitness and mental well-being. Exercise, like dieting, should start slowly and progress to tolerance under the watchful eye of a physician. It should also be tailored to each person's need. The doctor can prescribe an exercise regimen in much the same way that he prescribes medication.

Emotional Stress

Many people find it hard to understand how emotional factors, like anxiety, can have physical consequences such as increased heart rate and elevated blood pressure. The effects of emotional stress are very individual; the degree that is tolerable varies from person to person. Some people appear to thrive on high levels of pressure, functioning well and happily with a fast-paced life style. Others are more content with a quiet, peaceful environment.

The emotional changes people associate with stress range

from feelings of slight annoyance to full-fledged anger. When isolated stressful situations arise, the body is alerted by the brain to react automatically in what is often referred to as the "fight or flight" response. The endocrine system immediately produces hormones that, grouped together, are called adrenaline. These hormones, along with other natural responses, act to prepare every part of the body to protect itself. Some muscles become tense, while at the same time the blood vessels to other muscles relax so more blood can be pumped through them, carrying oxygen where it is needed most. Since the heart has the responsibility of pumping the extra blood to the muscles, it beats faster, and the blood pressure rises.

The physical changes brought about as the body prepares itself to face stressful situations are useful in their place. But when they are prolonged, as can occur with a poor job situation, a long-term family illness, or an unhappy domestic relationship, the results can be devastating. Since it is impossible to avoid stress altogether, one can only try to identify which situations create stress and determine how these can be minimized or avoided. Some other ways of coping with stress are to use exercise as an outlet, to talk out problems with someone, and to list priorities realistically and then decide which ones to tackle.

Personality Type

Certain personality types may be especially prone to developing heart disease. The best-known theory concerns the "Type A" personality, which has been defined by Drs. Meyer Friedman and Ray Rosenman in their book *Type A Behavior and Your Heart*. A Type A person is competitive, shows a sense of time urgency, and has an unrelenting determination to forge ahead quickly both socially and economically: in short, a person who wants to do too many things in too little time. This type of person is often a "workaholic" who takes little if any time to relax for fear of falling behind. The excessive drive to meet career and personal goals generally produces a great deal of emotional stress, which can elevate the blood pressure and result in associated problems. While changing a Type A personality (or *any* personality, for that matter) is far easier said than done, a person who is dedicated and committed to making the change *can* do so.

RISK FACTOR MODIFICATION

The fact that some risk factors *can* be changed should be regarded as good news. Although the habits of a lifetime are not easily surrendered, once he understands why a change is important the patient may be more willing to make the necessary adjustments to enhance the "new lease on life" provided by the operation.

It is not yet clear exactly what benefits will come from altering one's life style to eliminate or modify these risk factors. However, what *is* clear is that adopting reasonable measures and making changes where indicated cannot be harmful and may in fact be helpful in retarding the progression of coronary artery disease.

The key question is how to go about this task. For the patient who has just had his heart repaired, it may be helpful to regard the measures that must now be undertaken as a personal investment that, if wisely attended to, can only have a positive return.

Chapter Five

Diagnosing
Heart Disease

*First you go through one test, then another, then still
another. Pretty soon you find you're starting to root for
yourself.*

—IRMA L., sixty-nine years old

> The human heart has hidden treasures. In secret kept, in
> silence sealed.
>
> —CHARLOTTE BRONTË, "Evening Solace"

U NTIL HEART DISEASE can be prevented, the only hope
for its control is early detection, diagnosis, and treatment. Years ago, in order to make an accurate diagnosis,
the only things the doctor had to rely on were his own
observation and the patient's description of symptoms. As
time went on, however, major scientific and technological
advances in cardiology began to emerge at a rate that was
soon to revolutionize the field of medicine. Today, new
techniques for the detection and diagnosis of heart disease
are being developed at such a rapid pace that some tests
considered experimental only five years ago are already
obsolete.

What are these tests? How are they done? What do they

feel like? What are the risks involved? How many are too many? In short: What actually constitutes a reasonable workup?

Diagnostic tests for heart disease fall into two categories: noninvasive, which do not require that any device actually enter the body, and invasive, which include the insertion of catheters and other instruments. Although noninvasive tests are safer and less complicated, invasive tests, which usually require hospitalization, are far more detailed and accurate. Ideally, the combination of these test results can provide the cardiologist with enough information to make a meaningful diagnosis.

PATIENT HISTORY AND PHYSICAL

The first step in diagnosing heart disease is taking a medical history and performing an extensive physical examination. These are usually done in the office of either the family physician or the cardiologist. A medical history is provided by the patient, who reports to the physician on such items as past and present illnesses, family history of heart disease, and overall life style. The last includes information regarding pressure on the job, smoking history, daily activities, and personal background. Some of these characteristics have been demonstrated to be risk factors for heart and blood vessel disease and are helpful to the physician in making a diagnosis.

The physical examination includes an assessment of the patient's heart sounds, blood pressure, breathing rate, pulse, veins, and overall skin color. These can determine the need to continue with other laboratory tests such as blood workup, chest x-ray, and electrocardiogram.

NONINVASIVE TESTS

Electrocardiogram

The most commonly used noninvasive test of heart function is the electrocardiogram (EKG or ECG), which records the electrical activity of the heart. The procedure involves placing twelve electrodes (discs the size of a half dollar) on the patient's arms, legs, and chest. These electrodes are connected by wires to a recording machine, called an electrocardiograph, which prints out a tracing on paper of the heart's electrical activity. Some people mistakenly think an EKG sends electricity into the body. Actually, it is a device that *receives* tiny electrical impulses from the beating heart.

This easily conducted test yields some very important facts. For example, an EKG can precisely document the heart rate, that is, how many times the heart beats each minute. The test allows the physician to identify any changes in the pattern of the electrical impulses that may indicate heart muscle damage or heart disease that has occurred in the past or is occurring now. The EKG cannot predict what is going to happen in the future, however. An electrocardiogram may be performed in a doctor's office or in a hospital bed. It takes less than fifteen minutes and there is absolutely no risk or discomfort involved.

Echocardiography (Ultrasound Assessment)

Echocardiography is similar in technique to sonar, which is used by ships to determine the depth and location of underwater objects. The test provides exact and detailed information about the heart valves, heart muscle function, and chamber size. It can also document the presence of congenital heart disease. The patient lies on a table while a small microphonelike instrument is passed across his chest in a back-and-forth motion. The instrument projects harmless high-frequency sound waves into the heart and receives the echoes returning from the surface of the heart. The pattern of the sound waves is converted by a computer into an image of the heart's interior. In this way ultrasound can record the movement of the chambers and of the heart valves.

Phonocardiography

Phonocardiography simultaneously records the sounds of the heart and the pulse. To perform this test, a technician places one or more microphones on the patient's chest and secures them with small straps. The microphones pick up the sounds of the heart as it beats. At the same time, a recording machine draws a picture of the sound waves for interpretation by the doctor. A phonocardiogram helps describe the precise time events in the cardiac cycle and provides additional information on heart murmurs and abnormal heart rhythms. It is usually performed in a special soundproof room because absolute silence is required during this test.

Holter Monitor

The Holter monitor is a small device that is worn on a strap over the shoulder or around the waist and closely resembles a tape recorder. Electrodes, similar to those used for an EKG recording, are placed on the wearer's chest and the wires from the electrodes are plugged into the monitor. The purpose of this device is to obtain a twenty-four hour recording of the electrical activity of the heart. Sometimes the heart is monitored in a hospital setting, but most often the test is done as the person being monitored goes through his normal daily routine. The patient is asked to keep a twenty-four-hour diary of his activities: what he is doing and how he feels physically. The physician can then evaluate the heart's activity as it responds to the patient's overall daily tasks. The test is especially useful in the detection of irregularities in the heart rhythm.

Nuclear Scanning

Nuclear scans, which are also known as radioisotope studies, involve the injection of radioactive chemicals into the bloodstream for the purpose of measuring the heart's function without entering the body with catheters. The small amount of compound used for these tests is radioactive for only a few hours and can be safely circulated in the bloodstream without causing any adverse reaction whatsoever.

For the test called a radioisotope ventriculogram (also known as MUGA—Multiple Gated Acquisition), a technetium compound is injected into the bloodstream through a vein in the arm. The patient then lies on a table under a special detector called a gamma scintillation camera. The camera can follow the route of the radioactive compound, which is "attached" to the blood cells as they travel through the chambers of the heart. The test accurately measures the efficiency of the heart's function by allowing the physician to observe an image of the ventricle as it pumps blood from the heart. If damage has occurred to the heart muscle, the heart will not contract normally, and this will be evident on the displayed picture.

Some radioisotopes, such as those of thallium, have an

affinity for healthy tissue and will collect there. Other types, such as technetium radioisotopes, only gather in areas of dead tissue and can thereby identify the boundaries of heart injury. For a test called myocardial (heart muscle) imaging, thallium is injected into the bloodstream via a vein in the arm. A computerized picture shows the way it is distributed in the heart muscle. Since thallium migrates to live tissue, it is assumed that where thallium does not collect the heart muscle is either damaged or dead. The test pinpoints precisely which area of the muscle is not getting an adequate supply of blood, an important factor in assessing the degree of damage from a heart attack.

Another type of scan, called infarction imaging, uses the compound technetium pyrophosphate. Newly damaged heart tissue collects large amounts of the technetium isotope, causing a "hot spot," which can be detected by a gamma camera. Detection of the hot spot confirms a heart attack that occurred within five days of the test, the length of time for which the damaged cells will collect the radioactive compound. In this way a recent heart attack can be distinguished from old damage, which does not produce a hot spot.

Stress Tests

A stress test, or exercise tolerance test, is a means of applying controlled stress to the heart. The way in which the heart tolerates an extra work load provides important information about its functional state. An exercise tolerance test helps to diagnose problems such as inadequate oxygen supply to the heart muscle, heart rhythm disturbances, or impaired heart muscle function. These do not always present symptoms and therefore might not otherwise be detected.

For this test EKG electrodes are placed on the patient's chest and the patient is asked to walk on a slightly upgraded treadmill or, in some cases, to ride a stationary bicycle for approximately one half hour. Throughout this time the electrocardiogram records the electrical activity of the heart. The test can measure how much blood gets to the heart when it is needed. As a person exercises, his heart requires more oxygen; this test determines if the required amount of oxygen reaches the heart muscle as the exercise level increases.

As a safety measure, normal pulse and pressure rates are predicted for each patient before a stress test. The test is terminated when this point is reached or if symptoms develop. As the test progresses, blood pressure and pulse rate are measured to determine the effects of the physical effort on the entire cardiovascular system as well as on the heart. The treadmill starts slowly and gradually increases at three-minute intervals. If symptoms such as chest pain appear during the test, it is immediately discontinued. If the results indicate that the heart is not receiving enough blood for the increased demand of exercise, the patient is said to have a "positive" test result. Although one might think that positive means favorable, in this case it means that the heart is not functioning normally. Actually, the desired result from a stress test is a "negative" one.

A stress thallium test is a nuclear-scan exercise-test combination. The patient walks on a treadmill or rides a stationary bicycle to his predetermined peak point of exercise, based on age, sex, and what he should be able to achieve. At that point, thallium is injected into his arm. The patient then lies down on a table and imaging begins. A gamma camera scans the progress of the thallium as it accumulates in the heart muscle. A thallium stress test can document a heart attack or demonstrate evidence of coronary artery disease at times when a plain stress test is negative or inconclusive.

INVASIVE TESTS

Coronary angiography and cardiac catheterization are the most accurate diagnostic tests available for the detection of heart disease and the assessment of its severity. These tests allow the cardiologist to see what is happening inside the blood vessels of the heart without opening the chest. They are known as invasive tests because a thin plastic tube, called a catheter, is inserted into the body. This technique, however, does not constitute a major surgical procedure. In fact, the anesthetic for the procedure is local, meaning it is given only in the area where the catheter is inserted. The patient remains awake throughout the test.

Invasive cardiac testing is done in a special room called the catheterization laboratory, or the "cath lab." The patient is transported from his hospital room to the cath lab on a stretcher. He is gently transferred to a table that has a large x-ray machine above it and a television screen close by. There are usually five people in the catheterization laboratory for the duration of the procedure: a cardiologist, an assistant, a nurse, and two technicians. All of the staff wear sterile gowns, masks, and lead aprons that shield them from radiation. Since the staff members in the room are exposed to radiation many times a day, they must be careful to protect themselves. However, the small amount each patient

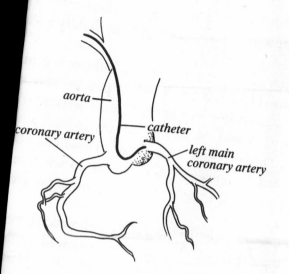

aorta

catheter

coronary artery

left main
coronary artery

FIGURE 16

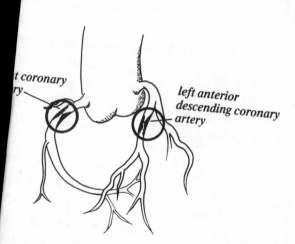

t coronary
ry

left anterior
descending coronary
artery

FIGURE 17

receives during the test usually does not require extraordinary precautionary measures for him.

Despite the fact that hundreds of thousands of procedures are done annually, cardiac invasive diagnostic procedures are not without risk. For those who insist upon numbers, a cardiologist might say that one patient in 1,500 develops a major problem during or immediately after the catheterization. Although problems rarely occur, they should nevertheless be mentioned. Possible complications include an allergic reaction to the dye, spasm of a coronary artery leading to damage of the heart muscle, and inducement of irregular heartbeats. Again, keep in mind that these are rare complications and in general the risk of this kind of diagnostic procedure is minimal.

Cardiac Catheterization

A cardiac catheterization is used to determine how the blood is pumped by the heart, what the blood pressure is within the heart chambers, and what the contents of the blood are as it flows through the chambers. A number of different techniques are used to perform a catheterization, but most commonly it involves the insertion of a catheter into an artery or vein in the groin area or the crease of the elbow. The area of insertion is first cleansed and shaved, then anesthetized with Novocaine. A special needle is placed in the artery or vein, and the catheter is inserted through the hollow in the needle. The physician slowly guides the catheter through the blood vessel into the heart. As he pushes it along he can watch the progress on a television screen that provides a fluoroscopic image of the body. Most people are surprised to learn that this procedure is essentially painless.

In fact, it is uncommon to feel anything as the catheter travels up the artery.

When the cardiologist has guided the catheter into the heart chamber, a special radio-opaque dye that can be seen on film is injected through the catheter into the ventricle. This may cause what feels like a wave of heat much like the sensation of standing in the path of an oven door as it has just been opened. The hot flash never lasts longer than one minute, however. As the dye begins to circulate through the heart, the lights in the room are turned off and filming begins. The process takes approximately one hour. The movies that result will provide accurate documentation of the filling and emptying of the ventricles so that the physician can observe different areas of heart muscle as the heart contracts and expands, and the way the blood flows within the chambers.

Cardiac catheterization is done without a coronary arteriogram if coronary artery disease is not suspected. Used alone, it is a highly reliable measure of congenital heart defects, valvular heart disease, heart failure, and other cardiac problems.

Coronary Arteriogram

A coronary arteriogram, as its name implies, provides information about the coronary arteries. To perform a coronary arteriogram, a catheter is threaded through the larger arteries and is ultimately placed directly at the opening of the tiny coronary artery (Figure 16). As the filming begins, dye is injected through the catheter into the artery, outlining the narrowing or obstruction and enabling the physician to detect its location accurately. Because the cardiologist needs to see as many different coronary branches as possible (Fig-

ure 17), he will undoubte
ent perspectives, turning t
tion.

When the filming is ov
from the body and an at
sional area until it seals its
the incision, and the patie
room. The procedure take
are asked to remain in b
catheterization. In genera
procedure.

It usually takes the labo
develop the films. They a
gist. The findings are disc
possible, usually within t

PATIENT SELECTION

There is no specific for
agree that clearly determi
surgery and who is not. In
surgeon to surgeon and,
patient. However, few su
operable or inoperable wit
and then discussing the de
colleagues.

The first step in makin
operate is to evaluate the p
information provided by th
and noninvasive tests. If t
heart disease, invasive tests
probably be recommended
A cardiac catheterizatio

right

right
arte

valvular disease or congenital defects and will clearly document the degree of the problem. However, the presence of malfunctioning valves does not necessarily mean an immediate operation will be required. Some people may lead lives with minimal or no symptoms for years before surgery is indicated. Therefore, timing of catheterization and surgery becomes an important issue for both the patient and his cardiologist.

When valvular disease is suspected, the cardiologist will look specifically for signs that indicate a change in the patient's ability to function. These begin with shortness of breath on exertion (dyspnea) and may increase to shortness of breath at rest. Eventually the symptoms may proceed to a point where the patient is unable to sleep in less than a semisitting position. Upon recognizing these symptoms, the cardiologist will probably recommend a cardiac catheterization to confirm suspected valvular disease and determine the degree to which the valve does not function properly.

If both the patient's symptoms and the cardiac catheterization suggest that heart valve replacement could significantly improve heart function, the next decision will be: *when* to operate? The critical time for valve replacement is when the disease has progressed to the point that it may soon result in irreversible damage to the pumping ability of the heart. If replacement can occur before the heart muscle is irreparably damaged, then the outlook is more optimistic.

Coronary artery disease is generally suspected when patients have chest pain or are unable to pass a routine exercise tolerance test. Either of these, coupled with a suggestive physical examination, may indicate the need for a coronary arteriogram. If coronary artery disease is documented by the arteriogram, the following things will be evaluated before the surgeon decides to do a bypass operation:

—Does the patient have angina (chest pain)? How severe is it?

—Is the angina stable or unstable?

—What is the degree of disability with exercise?

—Has the patient had a heart attack?

—If so, how recent was it?

—What amount of heart muscle is still functional?

—Is there a significant amount of heart muscle at risk of infarction, enough to merit the operation?

—Which arteries are affected?

—How many arteries are affected?

—What are the location and severity of the lesions?

—Are the arteries large enough to be bypassed?

—What percentage of the artery is narrowed?

—How sick is the patient?

—Is the problem likely to get worse without surgery?

—Is this the best time to operate?

A potential candidate for *any* cardiac operation is carefully evaluated in a process that involves combined efforts of the family doctor, the clinical cardiologist, and the cardiac surgeon. Answers to the aforementioned questions are discussed in combination with the facts obtained from the history, physical exam, and noninvasive tests. *Only then* is a decision made on whether or not to recommend surgery.

Chapter Six

Preparation for Heart Surgery

If you really think about it, the operation itself is only a part of the whole experience. I mean, it's not just the surgery that's important but also what happens before it and after it. And it's not just me who's affected, but the people around me as well.

—MILTON H., forty-nine years old

> The more extensive a man's knowledge of what has been done, the greater will be his power of knowing what to do.
>
> —BENJAMIN DISRAELI

SELECTING A SURGEON

The success of any operation depends to a great extent upon the skill and competence of the surgeon. Consequently, choosing the right surgeon is a most important decision. Some people have a great deal of confidence in their family physician or cardiologist and will leave the choice of the surgeon to him. Others, however, may prefer to participate in the selection of the doctor who will perform the operation. In either case, there are some basic questions that should be considered. For example, what differentiates a heart surgeon from other surgeons, and how can a patient find out how good a surgeon really is?

After medical school a general surgeon must have completed five years of training in an accredited surgical residency program. A thoracic and cardiac surgeon must complete two additional years of specialized training in surgery of the heart and lungs.

It is generally wise to select a heart surgeon who has been board-certified by the American Board of Surgery and the American Board of Thoracic Surgery and who is a Fellow of the American College of Surgeons. In order to be board-certified a surgeon must pass rigorous written and oral tests established and administered by members of the board. In order to be eligible for examination by the American Board of Thoracic Surgery, a surgeon must first be certified by the American Board of Surgery. Certification indicates that the surgeon has both the judgment and the ability to specialize in the field of surgery. Although it is true that there are some excellent surgeons who are not board-certified and, conversely, that all board-certified surgeons are not equally skilled, certification is still an excellent criterion of surgical competence.

The initials F.A.C.S. after a surgeon's name mean that the surgeon is a Fellow of the American College of Surgeons. While admission to the college does not require an examination, it is nevertheless a sign of recognition by his peers that his training, qualifications, competence, and ethics are acceptable.

Some people are reluctant to ask a physician directly about his qualifications. In that case there are other ways to obtain this information. In most local libraries two books entitled *The Directory of Medical Specialists* and *The American Medical Directory* are available to the public. These books contain pertinent information about each specialist, such as age, education, residency training, and the societies to which he belongs. Similar information can be obtained by calling the cardiology or surgery departments of a local medical school, or a local chapter of the American Heart Association.

It has recently been suggested in standards set by the National Heart, Lung and Blood Institute and published in the Federal Register that in order to maintain his skill, a cardiac surgeon should perform at least three heart operations a week. Every patient has a right to this information and should ask his surgeon about the frequency of his operations.

TALKING TO THE DOCTOR

The initial meeting of the surgeon and the patient before surgery may very well be the most important time they spend together. It is generally at this meeting that the foundation is laid for their future relationship, and it will help establish the patient's attitude toward the overall experience.

The surgeon's task is complex. He must explain the diagnosis, suggest what he feels is the best method of treatment, and give reasons for his choice. He should present the alternatives and describe the risks and benefits of all methods of treatment. Additionally, he should explain clearly what the operation involves, how long it will take, and what discomfort or complications can occur.

The patient has an equal responsibility at this meeting. He must provide the doctor with an accurate, honest, and complete medical history and description of symptoms: how long there has been a problem, what brings on symptoms, what relieves them, and how often they occur. This is also a good time to raise questions and discuss any concerns; there is no reason to be embarrassed or tongue-tied with a physician.

Listed below are some questions that a patient might want to ask in order to be well-informed about the operation and realistic about its outcome.

—Why do I need this operation?
—What exactly is the procedure?
—How will I benefit from the surgery?
—What are the risks of my not having the surgery?
—What alternative treatments are available to me?
—How many times have you performed this operation?
—Will you be doing the surgery?
—What complications can arise?
—How long can I expect to be hospitalized?

To the extent that the success of any operation is measured in terms of a patient's personal expectations, it is also important to outline for the doctor precisely what these expectations are.

THE SECOND OPINION OPTION

The "second opinion" has received a lot of publicity lately. The American College of Surgeons suggests that in cases where there are concerns or doubts about whether an operation is really necessary, a second opinion is advisable. In other instances, however, a conflicting opinion may only make matters more confusing. Actually, there are no hard and fast rules that say when a second opinion is needed. If, after discussing the operation with his surgeon and cardiologist, a patient feels confident that surgery is the best treatment for his existing condition and is comfortable with the choice of surgeon, then a second opinion is probably not necessary. But if there is any doubt as to whether the operation should be performed, it is important to seek a consultation.

Consultation has always been a part of good medical practice and a competent physician is usually more than willing to share the responsibility of such an important decision with a colleague. As a matter of fact, an increasing number of insurance companies are encouraging their clients routinely to seek a second opinion and will fully cover the expense incurred. It should be kept in mind that a second opinion is not necessarily better than a first opinion and whether there is agreement or disagreement, the final decision ultimately rests with the patient.

Selecting a Hospital

The choice of a hospital is usually related to the choice of a surgeon. However, an important issue in selecting a hospital is whether the hospital has the required facilities and staff for an active heart surgery program. This means that there should be a full range of medical specialists, experienced technicians and nurses, and appropriate support services.

To assure high-quality standards of patient care, the hospital should be accredited by the Joint Commission on Accreditation of Hospitals (JCAH). Accreditation indicates that all areas of the hospital have been recently inspected and have met rigid standards and guidelines established by the joint commission.

Federal guidelines suggest that cardiac surgery centers maintain a case load of at least two hundred open heart operations each year to remain proficient. This number is considered to be the minimum to provide the necessary experience to all operating personnel. A hospital's department of cardiac surgery should provide information, if asked, on the number of cases performed each year. In some states an institution's cardiac surgical center's mortality rates must be reported regularly to the state. If they are too high, the team's work may be reviewed.

PSYCHOLOGICAL AWARENESS

A diagnosis of heart disease and impending heart surgery can have enormous emotional repercussions for the patient and his family. Although each person may react differently, no one hears the words "You need heart surgery" without some degree of apprehension and anxiety. Two common responses to the diagnosis are anger and fear.

Anger may begin when a person feels as though he has been singled out to be the victim of heart disease, especially when he is surrounded by people with similar or higher-risk life styles who seem to have escaped this burden. For the slim, nonsmoking athlete who has just been diagnosed to have coronary artery disease, there is an obvious sense of injustice when observing a hard-driving, overweight chainsmoker who appears to be in perfect health.

Sometimes patients vent their feelings of hostility on their doctors, being upset that none of them has been able to find an easy cure for heart disease. Others feel safe directing their anger toward family members, who, after all, are usually the first to forgive and forget. If family members are able to understand the rationale behind the patient's behavior, it becomes easier for them to deal with it. They can also help the patient express and deal with his feelings more openly.

In some cases patients experience feelings of guilt and subsequent anger at themselves as they wonder if they could have prevented this. Some who were told to stop smoking did not. Others who were told to lose weight did not. Still others who were warned to slow down disregarded the warning.

Fears about being in a hospital and undergoing surgery vary in intensity from patient to patient. While for some there is great relief in knowing that they will soon be in the hands of people who "know what they are doing," for others just the word "hospital" brings about a shudder of apprehension. For most people, however, there is a common concern about pain and the outcome of the surgery.

If a patient needs support before the operation, it is usually available from both professional and nonprofessional sources. Although members of the family want to be involved, they often are burdened with their own anxieties. Most hospitals have trained personnel on staff who are aware of the need to discuss feelings and concerns. Included in this group are physicians, social workers, and hospital clergymen. Additionally, members from organized groups of postoperative open heart patients such as the Mended Hearts or the Zipper Club often are available to visit a patient. Since heart patients seem to identify with each other in a special way, a visit from someone who has been through the surgery is one of the best ways to offer needed reassurance.

NO SMOKING!

As a result of extensive campaigns to increase public awareness regarding the hazardous effects of smoking, the rate of cigarette consumption has declined measurably in the past fifteen years. Yet there are still too many people who continue to smoke. For years scientific studies have documented the connection between smoking and atherosclerosis —a topic that has been discussed at length in Chapter Four. Doctors, however, can do no more than instruct their patients to stop smoking. From there, each person must accept a certain measure of responsibility for his own actions. *Anyone* who is a candidate for surgery simply *must not smoke*! Assuredly, this is a difficult order for some who have a special need for cigarettes during this stressful time. However, it is essential that the lungs be as clear as possible before the operation.

The primary function of the lungs is to exchange carbon dioxide for oxygen. Tar in the lungs from cigarettes reduces the lungs' ability to perform this function. In times of physical stress or trauma, including surgery, when there has been a major assault to the body, the body needs all its strength for the healing process. This means that every cell must have as much oxygen as it can absorb. When the lungs do not function properly, the body is unable to receive adequate oxygen.

Another problem that results from smoking is "smoker's cough." As will be discussed in a later chapter, it is essential to perform coughing exercises during the early postoperative period in order to keep the lungs clear of mucus and prevent complications, such as pneumonia, from occurring.

The fact is, frequent coughing in the postoperative patient is uncomfortable because the incision is just beginning to heal and is still sore and tender. Nevertheless, coughing and deep-breathing exercises are mandatory parts of the postoperative routine, and must be done frequently. Unnecessary coughing, however, such as is associated with smoker's cough, is likely to put increased pressure on the chest. While there is usually no danger of the stitches opening, a cough may sometimes be quite painful.

BLOOD DONATIONS

One of the major advances in open heart surgery in recent years has been a steady decrease in the requirement for blood transfusions. It is still necessary to have blood available for transfusion, but whereas in earlier years many patients required eight to ten units of blood either during or immediately after the operation, today the patient usually needs no more than two or three units (one unit equals about one pint). In some cases, no extra blood is needed at all. When blood is needed, however, the amount required will depend on the circumstances during and after the operation. Therefore, it is impossible to predict in advance exactly how much blood will be used.

Many hospitals ask patients to have several people donate a unit of blood each before the operation. It is not necessary that the type of blood donated be the same as the patient's because the patient rarely is given the specific blood donated in his name; the donated blood goes to a blood bank, which credits the patient accordingly. Then, if transfusions are necessary, blood of the required type is simply taken from the blood bank as needed.

Having blood donated in a patient's name ensures that there will always be at least that amount available to him. If no blood is donated, a patient will still receive what he needs, but it will have to be paid for or replaced afterwards. Donating blood not only saves money but is important because blood itself is so scarce.

After surgery, the patient or his family is usually told how much blood was used. Then, if necessary, arrangements can be made to replace this amount in the future. If, as sometimes happens, there is a shortage of blood and not enough (usually four units) is available of the patient's type, surgery will be cancelled until the blood becomes available. One thing is certain: a surgeon will never operate on a patient without a sufficient reserve of blood to cover any emergency.

MEDICATIONS

At the time surgery is scheduled, the subject of medicines, both cardiac and noncardiac, will probably be raised. Any medication, over-the-counter or prescription, that is used regularly should be brought to the physician's attention, since it may be necessary to discontinue some drugs, such as aspirin, for a specified length of time before the operation. As a rule of thumb, no medicine should be discontinued abruptly nor should a new one be started without consultation with the cardiologist or surgeon. This includes cough medicines and cold remedies, arthritis medications, and tranquilizers. At this time, any over-the-counter medicines should be avoided if possible since they may contain aspirin products, which, like pure aspirin, retard the clotting factor in the blood and may cause postoperative bleeding complications.

Some cardiac medications may be continued even after admission to the hospital and should be brought with the patient. However, while in the hospital patients should take these medications *only as directed by the physician.*

TRAVEL

If, for some reason, a patient plans to travel out of town before the operation, he should ask his surgeon for the name of a surgeon or cardiologist to be contacted in the town he will be visiting in case any emergency arises. It is always advisable when traveling any significant distance to carry records that indicate exactly what heart problem exists, what medications are being taken, and who the primary physician is at home and a phone number at which he may be reached if this becomes necessary. Clearly, a patient scheduled for open heart surgery should never travel without first discussing his plans with his physician.

Chapter Seven

Costs and Fees

Thank God for insurance.
—SAMUEL R., fifty-four years old

A good heart is worth gold.
—SHAKESPEARE, *Henry IV*

H OSPITAL COSTS in general have reached the point where today a patient pays per *hour* what he paid per *day* in 1930; and costs associated with heart surgery are skyrocketing at an equally staggering rate. According to government figures, open heart surgery was performed over 200,000 times in the United States in 1981 at a total cost exceeding $2 billion, a figure that represents nearly 2 percent of the total health care budget. The cost of a single operation, including hospital and professional charges, can range from $15,000 to $40,000. The wide variation in these figures reflects the difference in the number of days spent in the hospital, daily hospital charges, fees for professional and ancillary personnel, and geographical location.

Costs for heart surgery are separated into professional fees and hospital charges. Professional fees may be further subdivided into surgeons' fees and those of the other highly trained specialists who are required to care for each patient.

Patients may expect to be billed separately by the surgeon, the anesthesiologist, the clinical cardiologist (the medical doctor who, in addition to the surgeon, generally visits the patient daily in the hospital), the cardiologist who does the cardiac catheterization, the family physician, and any specialists who may be called in for consultation.

As might be expected, fees will vary from surgeon to surgeon. Based on statistics published in 1980, the average surgeon's fees range from $3,500 to $5,000, depending upon the type and extent of the operation. For example, a single bypass takes less time and is generally less costly than a double bypass. Similarly, a single valve replacement is less expensive than a double valve replacement. Surgeons are generally willing to discuss their fees and if necessary may work out a mutually agreeable financial arrangement. It is best if this can be done before the operation, because it then becomes one less cause for concern during the hospitalization.

Hospital costs, which account for the largest part of the expense, are difficult to approximate because so many different facilities are used in the course of the hospital stay. Table 1 displays a sample of a hospital bill for an uncomplicated coronary bypass operation. Like other costs, many of the charges shown here will vary depending on the hospital as well as on the type and complexity of the operation and even on the geographical location of the institution.

Although insurance usually covers the greater portion of the cost of the operation, it is possible that up to 20 percent may be the patient's responsibility. It is a good idea for the patient to be familiar with what is covered by his particular plan because the type and extent of the coverage vary in

TABLE I

DATE	SERVICES RENDERED	SERVICE CODE	BATCH AND DATE	TOTAL	EST COVERAGE INS CO 1	EST COVERAGE INS CO 2	EST COVERAGE INS CO 3	PATIENT AMOUNT
	* * * * * * RECAP BY ACCOUNT * * * * *							
	1 DAYS UNIT	MED/SURG SE		2	156.00	TOTALING		156.00
	7 DAYS UNIT	CARDIAC MED		2	156.00	TOTALING		1,092.22
	2 DAYS UNIT	CORONARY CA		2	594.00	TOTALING		1,188.00
	* * * * *RECAP BY DEPARTMENT* * * * *							
	HEART SURGERY*			1,210.40	1,210.40			
	PHARMACY			477.10	477.10			
	RESPIRATORY CARE			54.70	54.70			
	RADIOLOGY*			246.50	246.50			
	PHYSICAL THERAPY			212.30	212.30			
	CENTRAL SUPPLY			1,699.20	1,599.20			
	LABORATORY			527.90	527.90			
	ANESTHESIA*			39.10	39.10			
	BLOOD BANK LAB			65.90	65.90			
	OPERATING ROOM			1,014.70	1,014.70			
	HEART STATION			105.00	105.00			
	IV SOLUTIONS			95.10	95.10			
	PACEMAKER			453.90	453.90			
	PACEMAKER			8,926.00	8,926.30			
	FLOOD GAS STUDY			385.50	385.50			
	UNIT MED/SURG			156.00	156.20			40.00
	UNIT CARDIAC MED/SURG			1,092.00	1,092.20			40.00
	UNIT CORONARY CARE UNIT			1,188.00	1,188.20			
	TOTAL CHARGES			17952.30	17952.30			
	ALLOWANCES			7,371.05-	7,371.05-			
	PAYMENTS			40.00-				
	OVERALL TOTALS			10541.25	10581.25			

*These are fees for equipment and supplies—not for physician services.

every policy, and it is helpful to know just what to expect in terms of financial outlay.

Common insurance plans are Blue Cross, Blue Shield, Major Medical, Medicare, and Medicaid. Blue Cross pays the hospital directly and may cover almost all hospital expenses except blood and physical therapy, depending on the particular plan in some areas. Because Blue Cross provides for a semiprivate room, patients wishing a private room, telephone, or television should expect to cover these expenses themselves. The difference in cost between a private and a semiprivate room ranges from $20 to $100 per day in most hospitals.

Blue Shield may cover a portion of the surgeons' fees (if the surgeons are "participating") and in some cases the medical doctors' fees. An established fee scale specifies the amount of money that the plan will pay. This scale is always available upon request from either the participating physician or a local Blue Shield office. Participating physicians in Blue Shield are reimbursed directly by the insurance company. If the doctor is nonparticipating, Blue Shield will make payment to the subscriber, who in turn will pay the doctor. In cases where a doctor's fee is in excess of what is allowed by Blue Shield, the patient is responsible for the difference. If payment will create a financial hardship for the patient or his family, this should be discussed with the surgeon before the operation.

Major Medical is a separate insurance policy that covers 80 percent of the costs not covered by the patient's primary insurer. For example, if a bill is $1,000 and Blue Cross covers $800, the remaining $200 is the responsibility of the patient. Major Medical insurance will then cover 80 percent of that, or $160, leaving $40 as the final expense to the patient or his family. Major Medical may also cover the costs of x-rays, special nurses, psychiatric care, and some prescriptions. Each company has different policy types that determine the conditions of the coverage, and these should be reviewed by the patient before surgery.

Medicare is a health insurance plan that is sponsored by the federal government. It covers all citizens of the United States who are sixty-five or older or who are on permanent disability. Medicare pays 80 percent of all professional fees according to an established standard fee schedule. Doctors who participate in the Medicare payment plan must accept the designated fee: this means that Medicare pays the doctor 80 percent of the established fee, and the additional 20 percent is the responsibility of the patient. A nonparticipating doctor will bill the patient according to his own fee scales. In that case, Medicare will pay the standard amount to the patient, who must in turn pay the doctor. If blood is necessary, the first three units are paid for by the patient or can be replaced by a blood donation to his credit. After that, any additional blood will be paid for in full by Medicare.

Medicaid, which is funded by the state government, provides for that portion of the population whose income falls below a designated amount. Professional fees and hospital charges are covered according to an established fee scale. Physicians and hospitals that are eligible to receive these payments have agreed to accept them as the final amount and may not submit an additional charge to the patient.

A Health Maintenance Organization (HMO) is a prepaid health plan. As with other insurance plans, an annual premium is paid for each subscriber, either individually or through his place of employment. With this type of plan the subscriber is entitled to medical care either free or for a minimal charge, depending on the HMO to which he belongs. Care is provided by HMO-affiliated physicians and institutions. If a patient requires a diagnostic test or surgical procedure not provided by his HMO, he is generally referred elsewhere; the costs are still covered by the HMO, however.

Private insurance companies usually have predetermined fee scales that provide for all or a portion of both medical and hospital costs. Payment is generally made to the insured person unless there is a specific arrangement to send the reimbursement directly to the provider of the services. Overall, the type of policy determines the type of benefits that will be paid.

Chapter Eight

The Preoperative Period

The staff paraded through my room, one at a time, like a cast of characters taking bows at the end of a play. They told me what they would do and what I must do. And as each one left I remember thinking over and over, "I must not lose the responsibility for myself."

—HOWARD H., fifty-three years old

Once a decision was made, I did not worry about it afterward.

—HARRY S. TRUMAN, *Memoirs*

NO ONE walks into a hospital without some degree of apprehension—unless, of course, he works there. Perhaps this is because it is a totally unfamiliar environment with new routines, new rules, even a new language; to all of this the patient is expected to adapt immediately. Unfortunately, no one can tell a patient exactly what will happen as he enters this foreign domain. But there is one way to make the hospitalization an experience less likely to arouse fears and anxiety. That is, for the patient to know before he is admitted as much as possible about what to expect.

Patients usually come to the hospital two or three days before open heart surgery so that the routine preoperative tests, such as those described later in this chapter, can be performed. Only those personal effects that are needed *before* the operation should be brought to the hospital because immediately after surgery the patient is transferred to the coronary care unit, where there is little room or need for personal belongings. It is essential to bring all medications (not just a list) that are presently being taken and any pertinent insurance information, such as Blue Cross or Blue Shield insurance cards. Most patients prefer to bring their own pajamas and slippers, even though these will be provided by the hospital.

Patients entering the hospital go first to the admitting office. Most hospitals assign patients a specific time for arrival, and so notify them in advance. For the most part, adhering to the scheduled arrival time assures that a room will be ready. If a private room is desired, it is wise to request it ahead of time. This can be done by calling the hospital or by asking the nurse in the physician's office to make the request. Private rooms, if available, can cost an additional $20 to $100 per day. Some hospitals mail preadmission forms that can be filled out and returned days in advance, speeding the admission process.

After the admission forms have been completed, the patient is escorted to his room on one of the nursing floors. A nurse from the unit will welcome him, familiarize him with the hospital routine and the equipment in the room, and then take his temperature, blood pressure, pulse, and respiration.

Within the first few hours of hospitalization a patient

may be seen by as many as ten different people, each of whom performs certain tasks. Although routines will differ from hospital to hospital, the following is a description of what *generally* occurs during the preoperative period:

The parade of people is usually led by the residents or interns, known as "house officers." These are physicians who are completing their training and whose function is to help care for the patient under the direction of the patient's own physician.

Patients in teaching hospitals also come into contact with an array of medical students, student nurses, and junior faculty. In a teaching hospital, the house staff interview and exam are standard procedures considered to be part of the residents' training in patient evaluation. Another standard procedure in a teaching hospital is "grand rounds," or teaching rounds. A group of doctors and students gather at the patient's bedside to discuss his case. Being "presented" to students does not mean that the patient is sicker than others, or that he has had an unusual operation or an unusual diagnosis, but merely that there is some feature of his condition that may in some way be instructive or help to reinforce previous training.

At some point before surgery, the patient is asked to sign a consent form that gives permission for the doctors to perform the operation. This form is a *legal document,* and its importance should not be minimized. "Informed consent" means that a patient is fully aware of the potential benefits and risks of the surgery and the alternatives before he agrees to it. Essentially, signing the consent form means that a patient not only has been informed of the pros and cons of the procedure but accepts legal responsibility for the outcome, to the extent that he has been so informed.

Usually following close behind the resident is the laboratory technician, whose job is to take blood samples (if this has not already been done in the admitting area). Blood is taken by inserting a fine needle into a vein in the arm and withdrawing a small amount of blood into test tubes. The specimens are immediately processed in the hospital laboratory. Blood is typed and cross-matched so that if additional blood is required during or after surgery the type given will be compatible with the patient's. The blood is also tested to determine red and white corpuscle counts and to evaluate the function of the liver, kidneys, and endocrine glands. Blood sugar and cholesterol levels are also determined.

In the x-ray department a chest x-ray is taken as a matter of routine. The chest x-ray is indispensable for the detection of numerous heart and lung abnormalities such as lung congestion, respiratory disease, and heart chamber enlargement. In addition, an EKG is usually done, but this ordinarily takes place in the patient's room.

The pulmonary or inhalation therapist performs pulmonary function studies that measure the breathing capacity of the lungs. Patients are asked to blow into a small plastic tube attached to a machine that measures the force and the contents of the exhaled breath. Teaching a patient proper postoperative breathing exercises and coughing techniques is an important function of the inhalation therapist. Certainly one might wonder why it is necessary to "learn" to breathe and cough when both have been natural functions for a lifetime. But the fact is that once the chest bone has been divided and later wired together, and the lungs have been exposed, coughing and breathing are not immediately as easy as they used to be. Within twenty-four hours after surgery, a patient must begin coughing in order to clear the lungs of secretions and to prevent the development of pneumonia. Clearly, it is easier to learn these techniques before the operation than after it.

Many heart surgery teams have a coordinator or patient educator, often a cardiac nurse, whose role is to inform the patient precisely what can be expected before and after the operation. The educational process generally begins the first day of hospitalization and continues throughout the postoperative period and even after discharge. It is obvious that each patient will have different educational needs, but these are usually assessed by the nurse-educator and the teaching plan is formulated accordingly. Sometimes she acts as an ombudsman, or "speaker for the patient," and can be called upon to solve nonmedical problems while the patient is in the hospital. Before the patient is discharged, the nurse-educator will provide postoperative information to ease the transition between the hospital and home.

At some time during the "preop" day a patient is visited by his anesthesiologist, who will discuss his part in the surgery and will answer any questions the patient might have.

Some questions that might be asked of the anesthesiologist are:

—Will I be given medication before I go to the operating room? If so, what is it and when will it be given?
—Can I be put to sleep in my room?

—What type of anesthesia will I receive during the operation?

—Will there be any side effects?

—Will I hear or feel anything during the operation?

—How long after surgery will it be before I am fully awake?

—What is your fee for this service?

The surgeon or his assistant sees the patient the day or evening before the operation to examine him once again and to answer any last-minute questions. Many patients forget some of their questions as soon as their physician enters the room. For this reason, it is a good idea to write down any questions or comments as they come to mind.

The night before surgery, the patient is "prepped" for the operation. He will be asked to shower and wash his entire body with a special sponge containing an antibacterial soap. Then the patient's chest, abdomen, and legs will be shaved. Removing hair from the body not only is an important measure that ensures a sterile operative area but also will make removal of the adhesive bandages much easier.

No later than 10 P.M., a small snack of juice and crackers may be offered. From then on, the orders are strictly "NPO," which means nothing by mouth. The only exception is the sip of water required to swallow the sedative that is given before bedtime. The sedative ensures that a patient will sleep well despite his normal anxieties regarding the pending operation the next morning.

Chapter Nine

The Operating Room and the Operating Team

The operating room has a fascination of its own. If anyone tells you it's exactly like you see it on television . . . believe him.

—LORETTA F., sixty-two years old

> A man's chest . . . open, his heart beating, a meditative heart surgeon looking in . . . That scene would frighten a child, fascinate a philosopher, send a modern art sophisticate back to his studio. A mighty sight it is up at the top of the heart.
>
> —GUSTAV ECKSTEIN, *The Body Has a Head*

THE OPERATING ROOM

As a rule, open heart surgery patients arrive in the operating room or operating suite slightly sedated but still very much aware of what is going on around them. Certainly from the patient's point of view it would seem to be better if a shot could be given in the hospital room that would put him to sleep and keep him asleep until the operation was over. But it is in the patient's best interest to be sedated for as short a time as possible, and there is always the chance of a last-minute delay causing a temporary "hold" in the scheduled time for the start of the operation. For example, the assigned operating room may not be ready if the previous procedure being done in that room has taken longer than anticipated. Or the surgeon may be delayed by an emergency, which always takes precedence over an elective operation. In cases like these, if the patient had been anesthetized on schedule, he would then have had to remain asleep and closely attended longer than was actually necessary, or be given additional doses of the drugs.

Since the patient will be awake, it is comforting to be familiar with the surroundings. What follows is a description of who and what a patient can expect to see before being put to sleep for his operation.

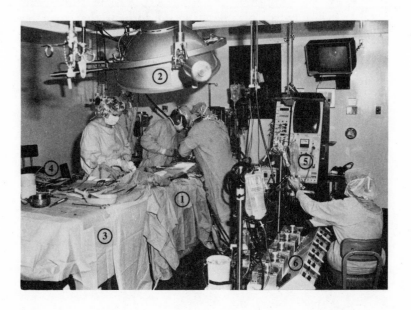

An open heart operating room is bigger than most other operating rooms because it must accommodate large amounts of equipment and a staff of at least nine people. The pieces of equipment that will be used during the surgery are described below and indicated by number on the preceding photograph.

1. The operating table is centrally located and is mechanically adjustable to any height and angle, thus providing the surgeon with maximum access to the operative site, i.e., the area of the body to be operated upon.
2. The overhead lights are of high intensity and can be positioned by the surgeon to give the best possible illumination of the operating field, to ensure that the exposed area is visible during the procedure.
3. The instrument table at the foot of the operating table holds pieces of operative equipment that may be needed.
4. Another nearby table holds the "software"—the large gauze pads called sponges, dressings, and bandages used during the operation. (All instruments and software must be accounted for before the chest is closed with sutures.)
5. The physiological data monitor, a sophisticated electronic device that resembles a five-screen television set, displays the patient's EKG, arterial blood pressure, venous pressure, and temperature.
6. The heart-lung machine is placed close to the operating table and is tended at all times by technicians.

THE OPERATING TEAM

Successful heart surgery depends upon perfect coordination and teamwork among the surgeon, anesthesiologist, surgical assistants, cardiopulmonary pump technicians, and nursing staff. As soon as the patient is wheeled into the operating room, he is transferred to the care of these highly trained professionals whose collective efforts are focused directly on a single goal: his well-being.

The anesthesiologist has the major task of maintaining the patient safely in a state of deep sleep throughout the operation. After putting the patient to sleep at the start, he gives constant attention to breathing patterns, blood circulation, and heart activity, and he administers fluids and drugs as necessary. As the operation draws to a close, it is his responsibility to regulate the support systems so that the body functions that during the operation were primarily maintained and controlled by medications can respond on their own. At the end of the operation the anesthesiologist accompanies the patient as he is transferred from the operating room to the recovery room or coronary care unit. There he will remain by the patient's side until the vital signs are stable and the patient is safely transferred to the care of the physicians and nurses in the coronary care unit.

In any operation, it is always the surgeon who is in command and leads the rest of the team. As the leader, he is responsible for the final outcome of the procedure. When the heart surgeon enters the operating room he is completely familiar with the patient's condition because only minutes earlier he reviewed the films of the patient's heart. Before going into the operating room, all surgeons and nurses who will be directly involved in the operation must "scrub" for the surgery. This is a procedure that includes a timed washing of hands and forearms with a disposable sterile surgical sponge soaked in special antiseptic solution. As soon as the surgeon enters the operating room he is helped into a sterile gown and gloves by the scrub nurse. He is now ready to operate.

As the operation proceeds, the surgeon performs the major intricate technical aspects of the surgery. He issues the directive to the pump team to go "on bypass," performs the surgery on the heart itself, and, once this is completed, prepares to take the patient "off bypass." At this critical point, when the heart must take over the function of pumping blood to the body, the surgeon must work in concert with the pump technicians and the anesthesiologist. Once the heart is safely beating on its own, the surgeon or surgeon's assistants suture the chest closed, bandage the incisions and prepare the patient for transfer to the coronary care unit or recovery area.

Most open heart surgeons have at least one, and usually two, surgical assistants. They are either senior residents completing their final year of thoracic surgical training or highly trained physicians' assistants. The surgical assistants work with the surgeon during the operation and are in a position to act as a "second pair of hands" at any time. It is their responsibility to keep the operative site clear, to hold retractors, to place sutures, and in general to respond to the surgeon's needs as they arise.

During the operation the scrub nurse hands the surgeon the sterile equipment and surgical instruments as they are needed. She is called a scrub nurse because, like the surgeons, she has direct contact with the patient and the instruments during the operation and is therefore required to perform the preoperative "scrub." The scrub nurse sets up the instrument and software tables before the start of the operation, and she shares the responsibility with the circulating nurse for the instrument and sponge count at the end. Contrary to stories commonly seen on television, leaving a surgical instrument or a sponge in a patient is extremely rare, because of the legal requirement for operative materials to be counted at least twice at the final stages of any operation. This is always done *before* the incision is closed.

In some hospitals the circulating nurse is known as the operating room manager. Her title "circulating nurse" is derived from some of the functions she performs, such as delivering specimens or securing additional supplies, which at times require her to leave the immediate operating area for a few moments. With the exception of the operation itself, she has responsibility for most of what takes place in the operating room. For example, she is responsible for the total operating environment, which plays a silent but very important role in any surgery. The temperature, the lights, and the electrical system must be strictly monitored so that the safety of the sophisticated equipment and the personnel are not jeopardized. The circulating nurse also fills out all the forms that detail the procedure as it is in progress.

The team of perfusionists operates the heart-lung machine, which totally supports the patient's life functions for at least one third of the operation. This allows the surgeon to operate on a quiet heart. It is the perfusionist's responsibility to set up the machine before each operation, a process that involves meticulously threading yards of tubing through the pumps. The perfusionist controls the flow and pressure of the blood as it travels through the heart-lung machine and monitors the patient's vital signs during the time the patient is on bypass.

Chapter Ten

Open Heart Surgery

I think the moment the whole thing really hit me was when they wheeled me into the elevator on the way to the operating room. It was at that very moment, sleepy as I was, that I realized what lay ahead. I tell you, it simply took my breath away.

—ROBERT A., forty-two years old

> True! . . . very, very dreadfully nervous I had been and am! . . . The disease had sharpened my senses . . . not dulled them. Harken! and observe how healthily, how calmly I can tell you the whole story.
>
> —EDGAR ALLAN POE, "The Tell-Tale Heart"

IT IS USUALLY EARLY in the morning when the slightly sedated patient is wheeled on a stretcher into the operating room. At first sight, the atmosphere is one of movement and efficiency, yet there is almost total silence. Masked, gowned, and gloved, members of the operating team await the patient's arrival. The surgeon dominates the room, speaking softly as he communicates with his staff.

The patient is helped from the stretcher to the operating table, and a clean sheet is placed over him from the neck down. The anesthesiologist voices his greeting, then quickly and gently inserts into the patient's arm a small needle to which is attached a tiny plastic tube. This is the intravenous (IV) line. The tiny prick from the needle is the only discomfort the patient feels, because anesthesia is administered through this line. Once the anesthesiologist is certain the patient is sleeping, various monitors are attached and the surgeon will proceed.

Open heart surgery can take from three to six hours, depending on the patient's anatomy and the type of surgery. It is best explained by separating it into five stages: inserting the monitoring lines; opening the chest; connecting the heart-lung machine; surgery on the heart; and closing the chest.

INSERTING THE MONITORING LINES

The first stage begins as the anesthesiologist inserts an endotracheal tube (breathing tube) through the sleeping patient's mouth into his windpipe, providing a direct channel to the lungs. The tube is attached to a ventilator (breathing machine), which mechanically regulates breathing and assures an adequate supply of oxygen to the lungs throughout the operation.

Just after the anesthesia is administered, a thin plastic tube called a catheter is placed in the bladder to drain and measure urine. This provides an assessment of kidney function while the patient is asleep. The catheter remains in place for a day or two after surgery or until the patient can urinate comfortably himself.

Three additional "lines" are inserted: one into an artery in the wrist or groin, and two into the large veins of the shoulder area. The lines are connected to electronic monitors that record the blood pressure in the arteries and veins. Blood samples also are periodically obtained from the arterial line to ascertain whether oxygen and certain blood chemical levels are within the normal range. The central venous line is threaded into the vena cava, the large vein leading to the heart. It is used to evaluate venous pressure and as a route for giving blood and/or drugs during the operation. Another catheter measures pressure in the pulmonary artery and is used to evaluate precisely how the heart is performing. Small plastic electrodes are placed on both sides of the chest and are connected to an electronic monitor that gives a continuous readout of the electrical activity of the heart. All of these data are displayed simultaneously on a console that provides the personnel in the room with an up-to-the-second account of what is occurring within the body during the operation. When the machines, wires, and tubes are all in place, the next stage of surgery begins.

OPENING THE CHEST

The surgeon makes the first incision down the center of the chest from below the neck to just below the end of the breastbone (the sternum). The length of the incision varies from 14 to 26 inches, depending upon the patient's size. The skin is separated, bringing into view the sternum, which is then divided vertically. The two halves of the sternum (connected to the rib cage) are gently wedged apart and held open by a metal retractor. This exposes the pericardium, the thin sac that encloses and protects the heart. Next, the surgeon carefully snips open the pericardial sac.

For the first time, the beating heart is exposed.

Connecting the Heart-Lung Machine

The principle of the heart-lung machine is simple. Venous blood returning to the heart is diverted to the machine, where carbon dioxide is exchanged for oxygen. Then the fresh, oxygenated blood is returned by the machine into the patient's arterial system. Thus the machine acts as a "heart" in that it pumps the blood, and as a "lung" in that it exchanges carbon dioxide and oxygen.

The machine is connected in the following manner: One or two plastic tubes are inserted through the right atrium into the two great veins (the superior and inferior vena cavae) that carry the blood returning from the body to the heart. Oxygen-poor blood that normally flows into the right side of the heart and then to the lungs for oxygen now flows instead into these tubes and directly into the heart-lung machine, never entering the heart at all. As it travels through the machine, the blood gives up carbon dioxide and picks up its supply of oxygen. It is then pumped out of the machine and returned to the patient by way of another tube that has been inserted into the aorta or another major artery. From there the blood travels along its normal course to the rest of the body in the usual way.

Only when the surgeon is operating *directly on the heart* is circulation mechanically maintained in this manner. At the moment the machine completely takes over for the heart, the patient is said to be "on bypass."

With the heart-lung machine in operation, the body temperature is gradually lowered by cooling the blood as it passes through the machine. Decreasing the body's temperature decreases its metabolic demands, similar to going into hibernation for a while. Patients are placed on a thin water-cooled mattress; adjusting the temperature of the water circulating in the mattress also helps regulate the temperature of the body by adding or removing heat from the body's surface. When the body temperature reaches approximately 86 degrees Fahrenheit, the heart slows down and may stop spontaneously. At this time a clamp is placed across the aorta just above the area where it connects to the heart, thus isolating the heart from the rest of the body. A cooling solution is injected into the aorta between the clamp and the heart that further lowers the heart's temperature to 70 degrees Fahrenheit, minimizing the heart's requirement for oxygen during the time the patient is "on bypass." Surgery on the heart itself may now begin.

SURGERY ON THE HEART

Coronary Artery Bypass Surgery

The purpose of bypass surgery is to restore the flow of blood to areas of the heart that receive an inadequate amount as a result of narrowed or blocked coronary arteries. Bypass surgery is sometimes called aortocoronary bypass (ACB) or coronary artery bypass graft (CABG, or "cabbage"). To accomplish a bypass, a segment of saphenous vein from the leg is removed to use as a vein graft. The vein is attached at one end to a small opening made in the aorta; the other end is sewn to an opening created in the coronary artery below the blockage.

There are several reasons for using the saphenous vein for the bypass graft. The first and probably most important is that the vein is autogenous (natural) tissue. Autogenous may be translated as "self-grown." Using a part of a patient's own body, even though it is removed from one area and placed in another, eliminates the chance for rejection of the graft.

Another reason for using this particular vein is that, like the appendix, it can be removed without risk, not being required for adequate circulation in the leg. In fact, when people have varicose veins, it is usually the saphenous vein that is involved, in which case it may be removed. And because the saphenous vein is close to the surface of the skin, it is easily accessible.

The vein is usually extracted through an incision that runs along the inside of the leg from the lower calf to somewhere above the knee. The length that is removed is ultimately determined by the number of bypasses required. Although only six to eight inches of vein are necessary for each bypass, the surgeon removes a longer segment so he can select the most usable sections. When more vein is needed, the incision can extend to the groin. After the vein is removed, the incision is sutured (stitched) and the leg bandaged. Sometimes a small rubber drain is left in to remove any fluid that may accumulate in the wound.

The surgeon prepares the aorta to receive the vein graft by isolating a small section of the aorta with a special clamp. Then a small hole is made for the upper end of each bypass graft. (Figure 18.) A separate segment of saphenous vein is sewn in turn to each of the small openings made in the aorta. (Figure 19.)

Next a small incision is made in the coronary artery *below* the blockage. The lower end of the vein graft is stitched to this opening. (Figure 20.) The procedure is repeated for each vessel to be bypassed. In some cases the internal mammary artery, one of the arteries that carries blood to the inside of

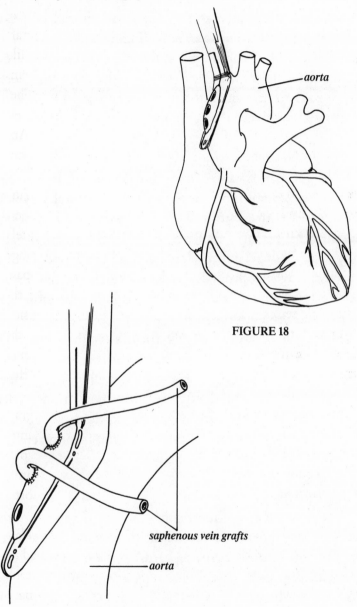

aorta

FIGURE 18

saphenous vein grafts

aorta

FIGURE 19

the chest wall, is used as a bypass vessel instead of (or in addition to) the saphenous vein. (Figure 21.)

When all grafts are in place, the clamp is removed from the aorta. Blood will then flow freely from the aorta, through the grafts, and into the coronary arteries beyond the narrowed or blocked area. (Figure 22.)

Valve Surgery

The purpose of valve surgery is to replace or repair heart valves that do not function properly. The natural valve can be replaced with an artificial one whose opening and closing mechanisms perform similarly. That is, the artificial valve acts like a stopper when closed and allows blood to flow through it when open. Although an artificial valve does not look like a human valve, it works in much the same way and functions almost as well.

Heart valve surgery largely focuses on the two valves located on the left side of the heart, for it is from this side that oxygenated blood, returning from the lungs, is pumped to the body. The mitral valve regulates flow from the left atrium into the left ventricle, and the aortic valve regulates flow from the left ventricle into the aorta, from where it is delivered to the rest of the body.

Valve Replacement

Today some of the most commonly used valves are the ball-in-cage, the disc valve, and the tissue valve (Figure 23).

The ball-in-cage (Starr-Edwards) functions similarly to the ball valve on a snorkel tube apparatus, permitting blood to flow freely when the ball is raised and preventing the backward flow of blood when it is dropped. The tilting disc

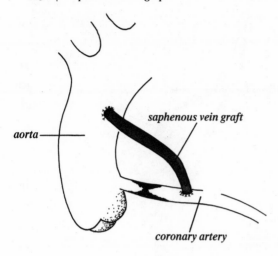

FIGURE 20

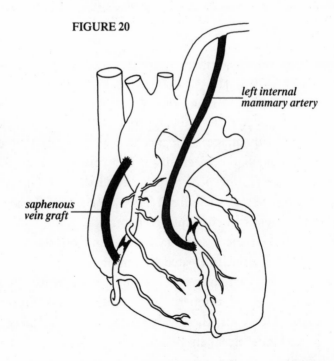

FIGURE 21

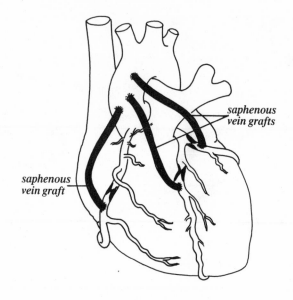

*saphenous
vein grafts*

*saphenous
vein graft*

FIGURE 22

valve (Bjork-Shiley) is made of metal and cloth. The disc permits free flow of blood when open and prevents leakage when it flips shut at the appropriate time in the heart cycle. The disadvantage of a mechanical valve is that clots can build up in the mechanism. For this reason, patients with these valves are placed on a blood thinner (anticoagulant) for the rest of their lives. This subject will be addressed in more detail in subsequent chapters.

The porcine (tissue) valve is taken from the heart of a pig and is chemically treated for use in humans. The reason for using this particular type of valve is that it usually does not require blood thinners, since there are no exposed metal parts. However, these valves can calcify and may begin to deteriorate after ten years, making a second valve replacement operation necessary. The porcine valve is recom-

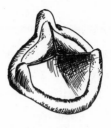

tissue valve   *ball-in-cage valve*   *disc valve*

FIGURE 23

mended for people in whom long-term anticoagulant therapy would be detrimental, such as women who wish to become pregnant.

Although the surgeon usually knows before the operation what valve he would prefer to use, he will make the final decision during the operation, when he can more closely examine the patient's heart.

In order to replace a mitral valve, the surgeon makes an incision through the left atrium into the heart to expose the natural mitral valve. He cuts away the damaged leaflets (or flaps) of the valve, leaving only the firm ring that supported them. The new valve is then sewn securely into position on the supporting ring of the natural valve (Figure 24). Aortic valve replacement is accomplished via an incision into the aorta itself, just above the aortic valve. Usually only one valve is replaced, but two or even three valves may be replaced during the same procedure. Occasionally coronary artery bypass surgery is combined with valve surgery.

Valve Repair

In general, mitral valve repair is preferable to replacement because it is simpler to do and because it does not require the use of artificial tissue. In cases where the valve is not severely damaged but the valve leaflets are too tight to allow normal blood flow, the surgeon will perform a commissurotomy, repairing the natural valve (without removing it from the heart). Various ways may be chosen to do this. The surgeon may free the tight leaflets by simply spreading (or splitting) them with his finger or by surgically cutting the leaflets apart. Commissurotomy is usually performed on the mitral valve but may also be performed on a narrowed tricuspid or pulmonary valve. It is rarely performed on the aortic valve except in newborn patients. Repair of a leaky heart valve that allows backflow of blood is done by partially sewing the leaflets together to narrow the opening, or by adding a piece of material to the leaflet to enlarge it.

Aneurysmectomy

An aneurysm is a saclike bulge in the wall of the heart, usually in the left ventricle. When an aneurysm is so large that it significantly decreases the pumping ability of the heart, it should be removed. The surgeon identifies the area of the aneurysm simply by observing the movement of the wall of the heart. After the heart has been stopped, he then cuts around the weakened area and removes the aneurysm. He may replace the removed tissue with a patch of synthetic

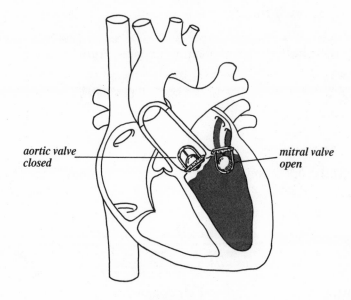

aortic valve
closed

mitral valve
open

FIGURE 24

material, usually Dacron, but more often he simply sews the
edges of the opening together. (Figure 25.) Aneurysmec-
tomy may be performed alone or in combination with
bypass and/or valve surgery.

Septal Defects

A septal defect, as discussed in Chapter Three, is almost
always a congenital problem, meaning it was present at
birth. A small opening in the septum (the tissue wall that
separates the left side from the right side of the heart) allows
blood to be shunted between the two sides. As with other
congenital defects, the symptoms may not become obvious
until later in life.

To correct a septal defect, whether between the atria or
the ventricles, the surgeon makes an incision in a wall of the

heart exposing the septum. If the opening in the septum is small, the surgeon may repair it by sewing the edges of tissue together; but when the opening in the septum is large, it is necessary to use a synthetic patch (Figure 26). New tissue eventually grows over both sides of the patch, which then becomes part of the heart.

CLOSING THE CHEST

As the operation draws to a close, the surgeon begins the process of taking the patient "off bypass." The blood is warmed as it passes through the heart-lung machine in much the same way that it was cooled; the water in the mattress is also warmed. The heart may begin to beat spontaneously or may require a small electrical shock to get it started. During this procedure the anesthesiologist, surgeons, and pump technicians closely monitor the vital signs and the electrocardiogram. With the heart beating on its own and the vital signs stable, the lines that connect the patient to the heart-lung machine are removed.

In some cardiac centers, temporary pacemaker wires are placed on the surface of the patient's heart before the chest is closed. These thin wires come through the chest and are easily and painlessly withdrawn before the patient goes home. During the early recovery period, the wires are helpful in diagnosing arrhythmias and may be used to "pace" the heart if, for some reason, it beats too slowly.

Two plastic chest tubes are inserted through the skin into the areas around the heart in order to drain off any fluid that might accumulate during the immediate postoperative period and to prevent lung collapse. The tubes are attached to a drainage bottle secured to the bedside. This is known as a closed drainage system.

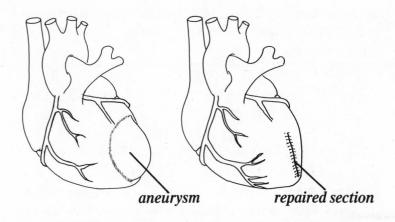

aneurysm   repaired section

FIGURE 25

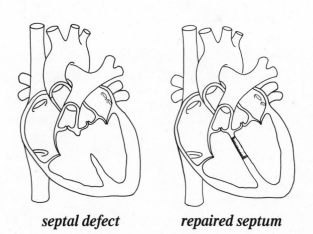

septal defect   *repaired septum*

FIGURE 26

The retractors that held the chest open are removed next. Then the surgeon brings the breastbone together with several small strands of stainless steel wire. The wires, which remain in place permanently, ensure that the bone will not shift when the patient moves about during the healing period. The sternum grows together in four to six weeks, much like a broken leg that has been set.

Finally the skin is sutured closed and is covered with a sterile dressing. The patient is transferred from the operating table onto a stretcher bed that has been wheeled into the operating room. He is then on his way to the recovery room, intensive care, or the coronary care unit, where he may remain asleep for six to eighteen hours.

Chapter Eleven

Support Devices

*What impressed me the most was the team's
cooperation. Each person was totally absorbed in his
own job—yet they each seemed to know what the
other was doing. Actually, I felt like I played a very
small part indeed.*

—KARL C., fifty-nine years old

> It is said that one machine can do the work of fifty
> ordinary men. No machine, however, can do the work
> of one extraordinary man.
>
> —CHINESE EPIGRAM

THE IMPORTANCE OF TECHNOLOGY in medicine has never
been so obvious as today. Two devices developed in the
last two decades, the intra-aortic balloon pump and the
pacemaker, are examples that have proven to be lifesavers
for some patients whose hearts require special assistance.

INTRA-AORTIC BALLOON PUMP

The intra-aortic balloon pump (IABP), commonly
known as the balloon, is a mechanical device that provides
gentle assistance to a tired or failing heart. When the heart
becomes weak or damaged, as can happen after a heart attack
or extensive heart surgery, it sometimes has difficulty pumping even the minimum amount of blood the body requires.

At this time the physician may decide to use a balloon pump to help the heart in the expectation that in time it may become strong enough to take over on its own again.

The balloon may be used in medical patients with severe angina, in those who have had a massive heart attack, or in those who are in shock as a result of heart failure. Shock is one of the consequences that occurs when the heart cannot pump strongly enough to keep the blood pressure at an acceptable level.

In surgical patients the balloon may be used preoperatively as a precautionary measure against any of the above-mentioned acute medical problems; or it may be used at the last stages of the operation if the heart has become so weak that the patient cannot safely be weaned from the heart-lung machine. In such cases the balloon may remain in place for a day or so to provide the necessary time for the heart to recover. The balloon is portable, so that when the patient is transferred from the operating room to the coronary care unit, the balloon console is transported with him.

The complete system consists of a console to which is attached a long, thin plastic catheter with a 10-inch by 3/4-inch polyurethane balloon wrapped tightly around the end. To put the balloon in place, the surgeon makes a tiny incision in the patient's groin over the femoral artery and inserts the narrow catheter. The catheter is threaded upward into the aorta until it reaches its proper position. A subsequent x-ray assures the surgeon that the balloon is in the correct place. Balloon insertion may be performed in any location as needed, such as the catheterization laboratory, the coronary care unit, the operating room, or even a mobile intensive care unit.

As pumping begins, compressed air is sent into the bal-

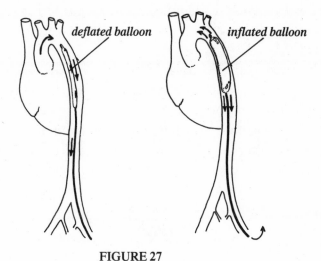

FIGURE 27

loon, which instantly unwraps and inflates to the size of a frankfurter casing. The fully inflated balloon fills 85 percent of the diameter of the aorta. When the heart is in the resting phase (diastole), the balloon inflates, displacing the blood that is in the aorta and forcing it into the coronary arteries and out toward the peripheral arteries. When the heart contracts (systole), the balloon deflates, allowing the blood to flow around the balloon. (Figure 27.) The balloon continues to inflate and deflate as the compressor pumps air into and out of the balloon in rhythm with the beating heart. The pattern of inflation and deflation is controlled by and synchronized with the patient's heart rate as determined by the EKG.

Patients may be on the balloon for as short a period as several hours or for as long as two weeks. During that time a balloon technician or nurse is in constant attendance to monitor the patient and the machine. The patient has little discomfort from the balloon itself and cannot feel it inside him. He cannot, however, move around to any great extent or leave the bed.

When the patient's condition has stabilized—that is, when the heart is strong enough to take over on its own— the balloon is removed. The surgeon simply withdraws the catheter, leaving only a small puncture wound in the artery. A nurse or doctor puts pressure on the artery for approximately half an hour, and the opening in the artery closes off. The tiny incision in the skin over the artery is then either stitched or closed with adhesive tape.

PACEMAKERS

As was previously discussed in Chapter Two, the system that controls the rhythm of the heartbeat (the pattern and number of beats per minute) is called the electrical conduction system. The normal heart beats rhythmically as a result of the transmission of electrical currents throughout the heart. If something happens to interrupt this chain of electrical impulses, the heartbeat loses its rhythm and may then beat too slowly, or erratically, necessitating the use of a pacemaker to monitor the beat and restore the rhythm to normal. A pacemaker is a remarkable device that consists of nothing more than a small battery pack (pulse generator) and one or two wires known as "leads." The pulse generator is an electronic power source that produces the electrical impulses sent to the heart. The leads can transmit these minute currents to the heart to stimulate it. These same wires also transmit information about the heartbeat back to the pacemaker so that it may turn on and off only when needed.

In some heart centers, every patient who undergoes open heart surgery receives a temporary pacemaker. Before the chest is closed, temporary pacemaker wires are placed on the surface of the heart and threaded through the chest wall. The wires are connected to a pacemaker unit the size of a Sony Walkman that contains the battery and the control box. The unit is usually strapped to the patient's chest or abdomen. In this way, during the early postoperative period, the surgeon can easily regulate the beat of the heart if it becomes necessary. The wires are removed by the surgeon before the patient goes home. This is a simple procedure and in general causes no discomfort.

When there is a permanent disruption in the conduction system of the heart, a permanent pacemaker is indicated. (Sometimes a pacemaker is used as a precautionary measure if medications that might cause a slow heartbeat are necessary to keep the heart functioning.) The pacemaker implantation is most often done under local anesthesia in a catheterization laboratory. The patient is placed on a table as if he were going to have a cardiac catheterization. In fact, much of the same equipment is used for both procedures.

A permanent pacemaker is the size of a pocket watch and contains its own batteries. The pacemaker lasts for as long as the batteries last. Once the batteries wear down (a process that occurs slowly and is detected within a safe period of time by regular pacemaker checkups), the old pacemaker is replaced with a new one. A pacemaker can last up to ten years if it has a lithium battery. Nuclear pacemakers have a much greater life expectancy.

The physician or technician prepares the site for the pacemaker implantation by cleansing and anesthetizing the upper chest area below the collarbone. A small incision is made to expose a large vein. As the lead is fed into the vein, the physician watches its progress on a fluoroscope that projects an image of the chest on a TV screen. The physician threads the wire through the vein following the path of returning blood into the right side of the heart. The fluoroscope allows him to see precisely where in the heart the lead should be placed. After the lead or leads are in the proper location, a small pocket is created in the same area (or sometimes in the upper abdomen). After the exposed end of the wire is plugged into the pacemaker, the pacer is inserted into its pocket under the skin. The surgeon tests the pacemaker to be sure that it is working properly. When he is completely satisfied, the incision is sutured closed and bandaged. The patient is then returned to his room.

Within a day or two after the operation the patient may leave the hospital. Thereafter, he may carry on normally, except that he must have his pacemaker checked at specific intervals as suggested by his physician. The time interval between battery checks depends upon the health of the patient and the type of pacemaker that has been implanted. The patient is always informed before discharge from the hospital how and when to have his pacemaker batteries checked.

Once the pacemaker has been implanted and the heart rhythm has been brought under control, symptoms should disappear. If they return, however, the physician must be notified so that the batteries and the pacemaker itself can be checked to see if they are working properly.

Chapter Twelve

The Early Postoperative Period

No one can really prepare you for that first glance at your husband . . . lying there asleep amidst a tangle of tubes and wires. All those machines really made me nervous at first. But none of the staff acted like it was anything at all out of the ordinary. I guess in a way that made me feel better.

—Mrs. Ira G.

The first thing I saw when I opened my eyes in the coronary care unit was the clock on the wall. It said 8:35 and it was dark outside. I remember thinking . . . "Hey, I made it!"

—Ira G., forty-four years old

> There is no feeling in a human heart which exists in that heart alone—which is not, in some form or degree, in every heart.
>
> —George MacDonald, *Unspoken Sermons*

THE CORONARY CARE UNIT

They say it absolutely overwhelms the senses. The sounds of hushed voices . . . machines, droning and whirring

. . . a blur of people in continuous motion . . . night, blending into day.

Be prepared for this. This is the coronary care unit.

And although at first it may seem much like a James Bond setting, it is in fact the *safest,* most *secure* environment in which a patient can be at this very critical time: the immediate postoperative period.

Unlike other postoperative patients, most open heart surgery patients do not go to a standard recovery room directly from the operating room. Instead, they are taken to a special intensive care unit (ICU) or coronary care unit (CCU) that has been designed to provide a continuous and systematic assessment of their physical status, with emphasis on the heart and its function. Here a patient is under the constant watch of medical personnel specifically trained to operate the special equipment that makes this unit unique.

Not all CCUs are set up in the same way. In some hospitals the medical patients (those who have a special heart condition or have had a heart attack) are in the same unit as surgical patients. In other hospitals, patients are separated into medical and surgical units. Some CCUs are wards, meaning the beds for both male and female patients are side-by-side with only a curtain between them. Others provide glass-enclosed private rooms that radiate around a central nurses' station. But the physical layout is actually secondary here; the nursing attention is the most important factor. And in most cases, at least for the early critical period, the ratio in the CCU is usually one nurse per shift for every one or two patients.

Feelings associated with the brief stay in the coronary care unit might best be summed up in the words of a patient who recently had a triple bypass: "At first, the thought of being connected to all those machines was terribly frightening to me. Then, two days later, the thought of *not* being connected to all those machines was terribly frightening to me." What happens during those first forty-eight hours to evoke such a response?

Upon waking up from surgery, a patient may be disoriented, sore, tired, and perhaps a bit confused. But soon a soft voice will be heard: "Your surgery is over. You are fine." This is the CCU nurse, the first person to bring order to this maze of movement and machinery. She will probably describe each piece of equipment as she uses it, starting first with the most vital piece of equipment in the CCU, the EKG monitor. Similar to the EKG in the doctor's office, this machine continually assesses the patient's heart rate and rhythm during his entire stay in the CCU. Electrodes placed on the patient's chest are attached by wires to the EKG machine. They pick up signals and relay them to both the monitor in the patient's room and a master unit at the nurses' station. Any unusual rhythm that may signal the onset of a problem causes the machine to sound an alarm and automatically to start printing a tracing of the arrhythmia on paper. Sometimes, if the patient turns too suddenly or if a wire becomes loose, an alarm may be tripped accidentally. For this reason some nurses will give a "false alarm" drill so that the sound does not scare the patient if the alarm should go off.

A bank of TV screens at the nurses' station continuously displays the heart rate and rhythm of each patient. A monitor is attached to each screen and is programmed to sound off if the heart rate becomes too fast or too slow. The monitor, however, is only one way the staff assesses the patient's condition. The nurse attending the patient will note his skin color, check his breathing pattern, and take his temperature, pulse, and blood pressure every fifteen minutes. This constant surveillance is one of the chief complaints of patients during the first two postoperative days, since the attention does not allow for any extended periods of sleep.

Another vital piece of equipment in the room is the respirator (breathing machine). Standing close by the bedside, it is connected to the breathing tube that was inserted in the patient's throat at the beginning of his operation. While the patient is under anesthesia his muscles as well as his lungs relax. Until the anesthesia *completely* wears off and the patient is awake enough to breathe for himself, he is kept on a respirator (also called a ventilator). As the respirator carries oxygen to the lungs, it makes a "whooshing," bellowslike sound. If there are any problems in the circuit, the machine emits a warning sound that will alert the nurse in the room to the fact that something might be wrong. The lungs are suctioned by the nurse through the breathing tube. The process of suctioning is uncomfortable, but necessary to keep the lungs free from secretions that if not removed can lead to pneumonia.

Because a portion of the breathing tube passes through the voice box, the patient cannot speak while it is in place. But the CCU nurses are expert at interpreting the motions of voiceless patients, so the slightest gesture can usually be understood. The nurse will probably offer pencil and paper to her patient so that he can communicate more easily. Occasionally the throat tube will cause some soreness and hoarseness, minor effects that generally diminish in a few days.

When the anesthesia has worn off completely and the patient is able to breathe satisfactorily on his own, the breathing tube is removed and the respirator is turned off. Usually patients are extubated within the first twenty-four hours after surgery. In some cases, however, depending on the individual's body tolerance for anesthesia, it may take longer.

To a horizontal patient, the intravenous apparatus looks like a suspended mobile of red, yellow, and clear plastic bags. Fluid from each of these bags reaches its destination in the patient's vein by way of the intravenous lines that were inserted in the operating room. The lines are used to administer blood and medications and to feed the patient glucose (sugar water). The arterial line in the wrist enables the blood to be withdrawn for daily blood tests without any discomfort to the patient.

In addition to the intravenous lines, other lines were put in place in the operating room and remain there in the coronary care unit. These include chest tubes, nasogastric tubes, the catheters, and pacemaker wires. The chest tubes, as described in Chapter Ten, are used to remove any air or fluid that might accumulate during or after the operation. They are attached to water-filled bottles that rest at the side of the bed. This closed drainage system emits a continuous gurgling sound that causes many patients to ask if it is raining outside. The tubes are removed by the physician before the patient leaves the coronary care unit.

The catheter that was inserted into the bladder during the operation remains in place for the first two days. It allows for an accurate measurement of urine, a necessary determinant of the functional status of the kidneys.

If a temporary pacemaker is used, the thin pacemaker wires that were placed on the exterior surface of the heart during the final stages of the operation are attached to an external pacemaker taped to the patient's abdomen. The pacemaker will regulate the heart rate should the need arise.

Some people are more intimidated than others by the equipment and find it harder to understand the concepts of the machinery. If for some reason the nurse's or doctor's explanation is not clear, the patient should not hesitate to ask for another explanation until he understands. Although nurses and other staff members are thoroughly familiar with the workings of the CCU, they are likewise aware that the patient is not.

To a large extent, the patient plays a direct role in his recovery. So much so that one CCU has a sign up in every room that reads:

ACTIVE PARTICIPATION IS ESSENTIAL FOR RAPID RECOVERY

Early movement is crucial. In fact, movement as soon as possible after surgery is one of the best presents a patient can give himself. It may be difficult at first but it clearly pays off in the long run. It appears that many postoperative complications that were once attributed to the operation itself were actually due to postoperative periods of prolonged bed rest. It is now known that a resting or immobile body slows down, becomes sluggish, and can be affected by shallow breathing and underactive lungs, both of which can result in pneumonia.

Immobility can cause a circulatory slowdown, which may lead to blood pooling and formation of blood clots in the leg veins. When swept into the circulation, these clots may interrupt the blood supply to the lungs. The inactivity of bed rest can also produce underactive intestines and constipation. And even something as simple as walking may not always be resumed easily after prolonged periods of bed rest.

In short, then, with the permission of the doctor, the patient's guideline should be: *Move, as soon as you can, as much as you can, as often as you can.*

This, of course, is easier said than done. The first step toward resumption of movement is being turned from side to side by the nurses. Until a patient can sit up, his body is gently rolled onto its side for a few minutes at a time at given periods during the early postoperative hours. This not only prevents accumulations in the lungs but also discourages tissue breakdown in areas of the skin or back that bear the body's weight.

The next step is to sit up in bed. This is begun as soon as the tube has been removed from the throat and the patient is breathing normally and without assistance. The nurse supports the patient as the back of the bed is gradually raised. This is a good time to wiggle the toes, move the ankles, flex the feet, and bend the knees, all of which help the circulation in both legs, especially the one from which the saphenous vein was removed. Surgical stockings will be placed on each leg to support the blood vessels while the patient is still in bed. After sitting up in bed, the patient proceeds to dangle the legs over the side of the bed for a brief period of time and then to sit in a chair next to the bed.

Coughing exercises, which have been described in Chapter Eight, are begun even before the patient sits up. A chest therapist may ask the patient to hug a pillow to support the incision during a cough. Coughing is also encouraged by pats on the back. Make no mistake—it hurts at first. And understandably so, since the chest bone has been split only the day before. But there is no cause for worry that coughing will break the stitches or cause the chest wound to open. This almost *never* happens. The breastbone has been wired shut and the inner and outer layers of skin are stitched firmly together. The chest is therefore quite secure.

Usually in the first postoperative day, the respirator and nasogastric tube are removed, the patient may sit up slightly in bed and a liquid diet is begun. By the second postoperative day, the urinary catheter and chest tubes are removed and the intravenous lines come out. The patient may then be bathed and also may move to a chair and even take a few steps. A diet of bland but regular food is started.

Pain is always a major worry of anyone facing surgery. Not surprisingly, people respond quite differently to pain. What is severely uncomfortable for one person may be regarded as a minor discomfort for another. After surgery, some patients complain of nothing more than awareness of the chest incision. Others are bothered by the incision in the leg through which the vein was removed. Still others report feeling as though they were "hit head-on by a Mack truck." Shoulder pain may be due to immobility in the operating room or transfer from the operating table to the CCU bed; throat pain may come from the endotracheal tube; and pain in the hip or side is quite often due to injections. Whatever the cause, there are many types of pain medications that work quite effectively and the prescribed dosage is not addictive.

Minor or major psychological symptoms may appear while the patient is in the CCU, but in most instances these symptoms are short-lived. The greatest problem at first seems to be disorientation, which is heightened by the strangeness of the environment and the large number of unfamiliar people wandering in and out, seemingly unaware that there is a person in the midst of all those machines. Part of the problem, too, is isolation; there are no phones, no radios, and the family can visit for only a limited time, all but eliminating the patient's link to the outside world.

At some time during the early postoperative period, a patient may experience a temporary depression that can arise from a variety of causes, most notably the physical weakness that places limitations on how much he can do for himself. Some patients say that this forced dependency on others produces feelings of incompetence compounded by a fear that the loss of strength may be permanent. This is a transient response, however, and it generally improves as the patient regains his strength.

As time passes, activities progress, tubes come out, supervision is less intensive, and the patient becomes less dependent on others to do things for him. He is able to walk around unassisted, can attend to his personal needs, and no longer requires continuous assessment of his heart function.

THE STEP-DOWN UNIT

After two or three days, or in some cases as early as twenty-four hours, the patient is transferred out of the CCU to a step-down unit. Despite the fact that every effort is made to ease the transition, transfer from the CCU is still met with mixed emotions. On the one hand the patient realizes that he is progressing well in his recovery. But on the other, he loses the sense of security that comes with being monitored continuously under the watchful eyes of a large number of doctors and nurses. This is why transfer from the unit can provoke feelings of anxiety or uneasiness, feelings that are normal and will subside within a day or two as the patient becomes stronger and becomes confident that he is able to care for himself.

The most common question about transfer out of the CCU is: Will the patient need a private nurse? In 98 percent of cases the answer is "no" because patients generally are not transferred from the intensive care of the unit until the physicians have determined they are ready to begin caring for themselves.

Some nursing units or step-down units have telemetry monitors. The patient wears a transistorlike device, either in the pajama pocket or around his neck or waist, that picks up his EKG and relays the signal to a console nearby. Trained personnel sit at the console to watch the signals so that the patient's heart rate is known at all times.

After the patient arrives in the step-down unit, activities increase, under supervision at first and then independently. Each day there are breathing and coughing exercises, weighing-in, physical therapy, and visits from the surgical team and cardiologists. Vital signs are still measured, only less often than they were in the CCU.

Some centers have physical therapy programs specifically tailored to the needs of postoperative open heart patients. The physical therapist conducts daily exercises and quite often can be seen leading groups of patients in bathrobes on a walk around the floor. Sometimes a written walking and exercise plan is provided, which can be followed at home as a continuation of those exercises that are done in the hospital.

Nutritionists and dietitians are fast becoming full-fledged members of the open heart team. They provide meal plans and teach patients and their families how to keep salt and fats to a minimum in the diet. As with the exercise plan, patients are often given diets to take home with them.

The length of the hospital stay varies with each patient. Under normal circumstances a patient can expect to go home from seven to ten days after surgery. But no matter how good he feels, the patient is never completely ready until he fully understands his medical condition and the routine he must now follow. Preparing a patient for discharge from the hospital involves cooperation among team members, the patient, and his family. A patient should know what to expect during a normal recovery, what kinds of late complications can occur, and how to conduct himself after returning home. The patient must also know what drugs to take, how often to take them, and what to expect the drugs to do.

Chapter Thirteen

Getting Back to Normal: The Recovery Period

> Patient: "Hey, Doc! Will I be able to play the piano after my operation?"
> Doctor: "Why, of course you will!"
> Patient: "That's funny . . . I could never play it before!"

T HE ULTIMATE GOAL of any treatment is for the patient to return to a healthy, full, and productive life as quickly as possible. Achieving this goal requires the combined efforts of the patient, his family, and his physicians. The greatest strides toward recovery are usually made within the first four to six weeks after leaving the hospital. But just as the hospital course varies from patient to patient, so too must allowances be made for differences among patients in how long it takes to get back to "normal."

In most open heart centers, postoperative patients are walking at a comfortable pace and doing simple exercises before discharge. These activities should be continued at home, increasing gradually as tolerated and as prescribed. It should be remembered, however, that recommendations for all activities must be combined with common sense for the best results and an uncomplicated recovery.

This chapter includes guidelines concerning various aspects of the recovery period. These are not the "last word," however. And it is advisable, if there is any confusion, to contact the cardiologist or surgeon for a more detailed explanation.

ANTICOAGULANT THERAPY FOR PATIENTS WITH VALVE REPLACEMENTS

An anticoagulant is a medication that thins the blood by slowing its ability to clot. It is mandatory treatment for patients who have had mechanical valve replacements, since a foreign substance in the bloodstream, such as an artificial valve, tends to encourage the formation of a clot on its surface. Since clots attract more clots, the eventual result might be the buildup of material on the valve itself, inhibiting its function.

The blood needs to retain at least some ability to clot so that a break in the skin, such as a cut or even a pinprick, will eventually stop bleeding by itself. Therefore the proper dose of anticoagulant (usually Coumadin) must be determined in order to establish a balance that allows the blood to clot enough to prevent hemorrhage, yet at the same time discourages a buildup of clots on the artificial valve. This is done by means of a simple blood test that checks the amount of time it takes the blood to clot. This test is called prothrombin time, since one of the substances in the blood that forms clots is the protein prothrombin.

Patients on anticoagulants have their blood tested once or

twice a week at first, to adjust the dose. Thereafter a blood test once a month is usually sufficient.

It is important to be aware that there may be side effects from the drug. If any of the following symptoms occur the physician should be notified:

—Blood in the urine (a pink appearance)
—Blood in the stool (a bloody or black appearance)
—Any unusual bleeding
—Unexplained swelling of any part of the body
—Nosebleeds
—Unusual headaches

Because anticoagulants are blood thinners, and because aspirin is also a blood thinner, aspirin or drugs containing aspirin should *never* be taken at the same time as anticoagulants without permission from the doctor. Also, if being treated by a dentist or any other person who might induce bleeding in the course of his work, the patient must be sure to alert him ahead of time about the anticoagulation therapy.

CARE OF THE INCISIONS

By the time a patient leaves the hospital, the chest incision should be fairly well healed. The chest bone may still be tender and the incisional area may at times become swollen, but it, too, is well on the way to mending. With normal healing it is permissible to bathe or shower at this stage, taking care to wash the incision gently and pat it dry with a towel.

After bypass surgery, it is not uncommon for the leg from which the saphenous vein was removed to become swollen at first because removal of the vein requires a long incision, and any incision tends to swell, however slightly, during the healing phases.

Three things are helpful in caring for the leg incision: the use of surgical stockings, elevation of the leg, and exercise, particularly walking. Surgical stockings are tightly woven elastic knee-length hose that support the leg without interfering with the circulation. Their gentle compression helps to prevent fluid from accumulating. They are used early in the postoperative period while the patient is still in the coronary care unit. It is usually best to continue to wear the stockings for a few weeks, particularly on the operated leg.

As often as possible, especially during the first few weeks, patients should try to elevate the leg from which the vein was removed. One way to do this is to place the leg on a chair when sitting. This will help to keep blood from pooling and the leg from swelling.

DIET

Although it is difficult to suggest diets that are appropriate to everyone, there is no question that the primary goal of most nutritionists or physicians concerned with heart disease is to help prevent or slow down the development of atherosclerosis. And the fact that books, seminars, and classes on the subject have proliferated to the degree they have indicates that the public is becoming increasingly concerned about the effects of diet on the body. The continual bombardment of conflicting dietary advice has understandably caused many people to give up trying to make sense of most of it. But there is finally some good news in that more and more of these reports are beginning to sound alike, probably because an increasing number of scientific studies is coming to similar conclusions.

There is now enough persuasive evidence to justify issuing authoritative reports. In one study, reported in 1982 by the American Heart Association (AHA) in the medical journal *Circulation,* the AHA outlined dietary recommendations designed to lower the risk of developing coronary heart disease in people with no previous history of the disease and to retard the progression in those who do have it.

The AHA recommendations are based upon animal experiments, population studies, and clinical trials, all of which provide "highly suggestive evidence" that diet can indeed affect the progress of heart disease. The report states that saturated fats and cholesterol in the diet can raise the cholesterol level in the blood (an elevated cholesterol level is a contributor to the development of atherosclerosis and heart disease). It places the recommended level of serum cholesterol at about 230 mg or less.

According to the report, modification in the diet should be made in order to reduce the risk of heart disease. Suggested ways of doing this are as follows:

· *Reduce the total amount of fat in the diet to a maximum of 30 percent of the daily food intake.* Currently the average amount of fat in the diet of Americans is 40 percent. In order to achieve the desired reduction, however, it is not necessary to give up the foods that contain fat. Instead, the reduction can be accomplished by making certain dietary adjustments: eating less of foods with high fat content or selecting foods with lower fat content to replace them. Examples of such substitutions include:

Lean cuts of beef	INSTEAD OF	Fatty cuts of meat,
or cold cuts,		bacon, or organ foods
chicken (skinned),		
veal, turkey, or fish		
Fat-free milk		Whole milk
Skim-milk		Butter or eggs
dairy products		
Yogurt		Ice cream
Low-fat cheeses		Whole-milk cheeses
Tuna packed in water		Tuna packed in oil
Fruit		Pastries

· *Reduce saturated fat.*   Saturated fats are usually those that are solid at room temperature. Currently these fats are found in 15 to 17 percent of the average American diet. But the American Heart Association suggests that in a modified diet these fats should represent only 10 percent of the diet. Meat, animal fat, butter, whole-milk dairy products, hydrogenated shortenings, coconut and palm oils, and baked goods are some of the foods that contain high levels of saturated fats.

· *Substitute polyunsaturated fat.*   Polyunsaturated fats are liquid at room temperature. Examples of polyunsaturated fats include margarine (only that which lists a polyunsaturated oil as its first ingredient), vegetable oils, and corn, soy, and safflower oils. The American Heart Association suggests keeping unsaturated fat levels under 10 percent of the diet.

· *Increase carbohydrates.*   Currently, 45 percent of most American diets consists of carbohydrates. To compensate for the decrease in recommended fats it is suggested that complex carbohydrates be increased to 55 percent of the calories included in the daily diet. These types of food add fiber to the system, which helps elimination, and they may help lower cholesterol levels. Carbohydrates can be found in foods such as fresh vegetables, fresh fruits, whole grain products, enriched cereals, and beans.

· *Reduce the amount of cholesterol in the diet.* At present the average American intake is approximately 450–500 mg of cholesterol per day. This is added to the amount produced in the body. The American Heart Association Committee recommends reducing the intake to under 300 mg of cholesterol per day. This would essentially relegate the medium-sized egg (which contains 250 mg) to the status of a dietary *treat*. It is helpful to avoid foods high in cholesterol. Most notably these include eggs, fatty red meats, organ meats (such as liver), shrimp and oysters, and whole-milk dairy products.

· *Maintain a recommended body weight.* It was shown in Chapter Four that weight reduction can decrease the level of cholesterol in the blood. It may also lower blood pressure and improve glucose tolerance, which helps prevent or control diabetes.

It cannot be stressed strongly enough that patients who are overweight should *diet only under their physician's supervision.* "Fad" diets, which are practically a way of life for millions of Americans each year, may help to shed pounds fast—but those pounds rarely stay off. In fact, the only permanent result from a quick-weight-loss diet seems to be a reduction in the pocketbook. The obvious answer to a problem of overweight is to eat less, eat properly, and exercise. Tips to help with weight reduction may be found in the section on weight at the end of this chapter.

· *Reduce salt intake.* The chemical components of salt are sodium and chloride. It is the sodium in the diet that increases water retention in the tissues. Excess fluid in the blood and tissues creates extra work for the heart, which must circulate this fluid around the body. One way to reduce sodium in the diet is not to add salt to food while cooking or eating. Many foods already contain large amounts of sodium either in their natural state or as part of their processing; people on a salt-restricted diet should read labels before buying processed or packaged food. Foods to be eaten judiciously (or avoided altogether) are lunch meats such as salami and bologna, smoked meats such as ham, bacon, sausage, or corned beef, canned foods that list salt on their labels, packaged bouillon, and condiments such as catsup, chili sauce, mustard, and barbeque sauce. Clearly, the best way to avoid salt is to buy and cook as many *fresh* foods as possible.

Changing dietary habits that have existed for years obviously cannot be accomplished in a day. For the patient who must now decide which changes he will make, there is an unlimited spectrum of choices. Making the right decision requires a knowledge of what foods are significant, which substitutions are beneficial, and what the caloric and nutritional values are for various foods. A dietician is usually available in the hospital to help with meal plans and menus. Yet success is likely only if there is a clear understanding of why the diet must be modified and a willingness on the part of the patient and his family to undertake these changes at home.

Driving

Patients often ask, "If I can ride in a car immediately after my hospital discharge, why can't I drive for six weeks?" The answer is that when the patient is driving, the chest is near a hard object, namely the steering wheel. In an accident or sudden stop, contact between the steering wheel and the breastbone can disturb the healing process. It is the bone, not the heart, that is in jeopardy. Seat belts should be used. When riding for extended periods of time the patient should stop and stretch every hour to stimulate circulation and prevent swelling of the legs, especially the leg from which the saphenous vein was removed.

Emotional Impact

It is normal for open heart surgery to take an emotional toll, however minor, on most patients. Some doctors attribute this to a temporary change in body chemistry resulting from the physical stress of the operation. Others feel that it may be due to the sudden realization of what the body and the heart have gone through.

Periods of depression, if they occur at all, are most common on the fourth and fifth days; occasionally they may not surface until the patient returns home. Being away from the immediate care of the doctors or nurses and the protective environment of the hospital sometimes plays a role. A recovering patient may have days when he will be "blue" for no apparent reason. Whatever the cause, these feelings should be accepted as part of the normal recovery process following any operation. If depression persists more than a week or two, however, the doctor should be consulted.

Emotional recovery may be hastened in a number of ways:

—Talk out the concerns with close family and friends.
—Keep busy at activities that are not too physically taxing.
—Get up and out of bed in the morning, get dressed, and stay dressed all day.
—Begin a walking program—exercise is a wonderful chaser of the blues.
—Remember that this is an emotionally trying time for the family, too.

Patients who are not forewarned may become fearful that they are not adjusting to the transition as well as everyone else. Therefore, it is important to know that such feelings can arise at any time in the early postoperative period, and not to allow this reaction to interfere with normal recovery.

EXERCISE

An increasing number of hospitals are including physical therapists on their cardiac surgery teams. Under their watchful guidance, postoperative patients participate in fitness programs that include walking, early range-of-motion exercises, and sometimes climbing hospital steps. At discharge, patients often are given written guidelines for continuing and progressive physical exercise, or such a program may be established with the physician at the first postoperative checkup. In any case, a postoperative program should be as carefully prescribed as the postoperative drug régime.

Exercise programs started in the hospital and continued

through convalescence may help a patient reduce depression should it occur. At home, along with the gradual improvement in physical well-being and a return of strength, the patient becomes more confident and begins to see himself as he was prior to his illness.

Walking is usually the exercise recommended for patients in the early postoperative weeks because it improves muscle tone and is generally relaxing. Some important things to keep in mind with the graduated walking program are:

—Set realistic goals. Patients should not compete with each other. Exercise capabilities, like the operation itself, are different for each person.

—Call the doctor if palpitations or unexpected chest pain occur when walking.

—Walking uphill, upstairs, or against a cold wind requires extra effort and makes the heart work harder.

—Eating large meals puts added stress on the heart. It is best to eat small and frequent meals and to wait at least one hour after eating before exercising.

—Sudden effort or exertion in high altitudes, high humidity, and extreme temperatures puts added strain on the heart. These conditions should be taken into consideration when exercise is planned.

—At the first sign of fatigue, *stop* and *rest*. If the fatigue continues, cease exercising for that day.

Sometimes, for no obvious reason, there will be an isolated day or two when exercising is more difficult. This is normal and should be expected.

FAMILY RESPONSE

Although family members do not personally experience the physical trauma of open heart surgery, the operation nevertheless can put a strain on their emotions. While the operation is under way they are concerned about the immediate outcome. As the patient begins to recover, family members are compelled to put everything aside and spend most of the day and early evening in a CCU waiting room, nervously awaiting the three or four intervals of short visitation. Many loved ones report their own feeling of isolation that comes from "taking a back seat" while strangers minister to the patient.

Often a patient's attitude toward his recuperation is reflected in the way his family and friends treat him. An overprotective spouse can easily reinforce the patient's feeling of weakness and incompetence. Or an anxious spouse can trigger anxiety in the patient. Whenever possible, stress should be kept at a minimum. Sometimes it is better to let the patient determine his own limitations than to argue with him about his activity.

HOUSEWORK, GARDENING, LIFTING

Like all other physically taxing activities, activities around the house should be undertaken gradually. Vacuuming, bed-making and gardening should be avoided for at least the first four weeks. It is best to avoid lifting anything heavier than ten pounds for the first six weeks. This includes bags of groceries, which can be deceptively heavy. Patients should be careful not to strain while opening heavy car doors, pushing "light" gardening equipment or even unscrewing tight jar lids, as these actions tend to put stress on the chest incision.

MEDICINES

Some patients will still require medicine after open heart surgery. Today, more than ever, patients are expected to play an active role in their own medical management. They are usually told by the doctor precisely what their prescribed medications are and what each one does. Patients are often asked to help in evaluating the effects of the medicine on themselves. Because medicines affect people differently, they may cause side effects in some and not in others. It is also possible to have an allergic reaction to a drug at any time. If any side effects or allergic reactions occur *the doctor should be contacted immediately*.

Listed here are some general guidelines for patients on drug therapy:

—Take *only* the drugs prescribed by the physician.

—Never stop a medicine without first consulting the physician. (Stopping some drugs abruptly may be dangerous.) Feeling better is never an excuse to reduce a dosage or to discontinue it.

—Never take two doses of medicine if for some reason one dose is missed. If pills are lost and several doses missed, the doctor should be notified, or the pharmacist consulted.

—Never take another person's medicine.

—Ask the pharmacist about the shelf-life of the drug—that is, how long the drug's ingredients remain active. These dates should be included on the label of each drug, as should its name and instructions for use.

—Reorder medicines before they run out, in case the pharmacist does not have a sufficient quantity on hand.

—Question the doctor about possible side effects that can be anticipated.

—Report any unusual reactions to the physician.

Table 2 lists common heart medications.

PREVENTION OF VALVE INFECTIONS

Patients who have had valve replacement surgery are susceptible to infection in and around the area of the new valve. Body tissues normally contain cells that resist bacteria, but an artificial valve is not made of natural tissue and therefore does not possess bacterial-resistant properties. Bacteria can lodge on the new valve, causing an inflammation known as bacterial endocarditis. To prevent this complication, patients are put on prophylactic antibiotics. This means that antibiotics are taken *before* any other operative procedure is done that might allow bacteria to enter the bloodstream. A patient who plans to have dental work or any type of procedure that may cause a break in the skin should notify the heart physician a few days before the scheduled appointment. The doctor may want to put the patient on antibiotics.

RETURN TO WORK

Returning to work usually depends on two considerations: how quickly the patient recovers from the operation and to what type of job he will be returning. It is always wise to wait until after the six-week checkup with the doctor before returning to work.

TABLE 2

TYPE OF DRUG AND GENERIC OR BRAND NAME	WHY OR WHEN NEEDED	WHAT IT DOES	POSSIBLE SIDE EFFECTS
Cardiotonic: Digoxin Lanoxin	Heart failure, poor pumping ability (weak heart), arrhythmias	Strengthens the pumping action of the heart, allows more blood to be pumped per beat	Decreased appetite, nausea, arrhythmias, tiredness, visual disturbances
Diuretics: Aldactone Edecrin HydroDIURIL Lasix	Heart failure causing too much fluid in the body	Removes excess fluid from the body by increasing production of urine	Dehydration, dizziness, potassium depletion, muscle cramps, arrhythmias
Antiarrhythmics: Dilantin Inderal Lanoxin Norpace Pronestyl	To control arrhythmias	Regulates the heart rate and rhythm	Fatigue, skin rash
Anticoagulants: Aspirin Coumadin Persantine	After heart attack or valve surgery	Decreases the ability of blood to clot	Excessive bleeding
Beta-Blockers: Corgard Inderal Lopressor	To reduce work load of heart, control heart rhythm and high blood pressure	Decreases blood pressure and heart rate	Shortness of breath, upset stomach
Calcium Antagonists: Isoptin Procardia	Anginal pain and coronary spasm	Relaxes coronary arteries	Headache
Vasodilators: Apresoline Cardilate Isordil Minipress Nitro-Bid Nitroglycerin Sorbitrate	Anginal pain and heart failure	Widens or relaxes vessels, reduces pressure against which the heart must pump	Headache, weakness, low blood pressure

Tranquilizers:			
Librium	Anxiety	Relieves anxiety	Drowsiness
Miltown	and stress		
Valium			
Antihypertensives:			
Aldomet	High blood	Lowers blood	Dizziness and
Apresoline	pressure	pressure	weakness, muscle
Catapres			cramps
Inderal			
Ismelin			
Anticholesterol:			
Atromid-S	Elevated	Lowers	Digestive upset
Questran	cholesterol	cholesterol	
		level	
Antibiotics:			
Too numerous	To prevent or	Prevents or	Drowsiness,
to identify	treat infection	clears up	stomach upset
	on valves	infection	

Some general recommendations are:

—If possible, try to resume job functions slowly. For example, try to work for only a half day at first and then gradually extend the workday to a full day.

—Base the plan for return to work on the physical requirements of the job. Obviously one can return to a sedentary or desk job sooner than to one that is physically taxing.

—If the job requires an excessive amount of physical labor, consider choosing a new occupation.

—If the job generates a great deal of mental tension and stress, you may want to reassess your situation before returning to work.

—If you cannot return to your former job because of the aforementioned reasons, or because the employer has discharged you, contact the vocational rehabilitation department of your state or local government.

SEXUAL RELATIONS

There is absolutely no reason why a sexual relationship that was satisfactory before heart surgery should not resume after the operation. Yet many patients, and not surprisingly just as many of their partners, are afraid of how sex will affect the newly repaired heart. An increase in heart activity during intercourse will occur but is not to be feared. A good rule of thumb is: if a person can comfortably climb two flights of stairs without difficulty, or walk three blocks briskly, he is ready to resume sexual activity, because both of these activities simulate the increased heart rate experienced during intercourse. Some patients are afraid the bypass graft will "break" if they become overly excited. *This never happens.* It should be mentioned, though, that extramarital sex, sex with a person much younger than the patient, or sex with a new partner *can* put added stress on the heart.

Sometimes postoperative sexual difficulties are the result of poor communication between partners. A partner has no way of knowing what does or does not hurt the patient and unless specifically told is sometimes afraid to do anything at all. The importance of freely discussing fears and concerns with each other cannot be stressed enough.

Resumption of sexual activity should, like all physical activities, begin gradually. Perhaps it is best to start with gentle caresses as a beginning to the physical renewal. Some positions are more comfortable than others for the patient to start with. They include the side-by-side position and "active partner" on top. Both of these should require a minimal amount of effort from the patient. As with all physically taxing activities, sexual activity should not be initiated within two hours after a large meal or heavy drinking because the heart works harder during the digestive process. And it is best if the patient is not tired or under emotional stress because these, too, cause the heart to beat faster. Once begun, sex should be stopped if the patient begins to experience angina or palpitations. Wait for these symptoms to subside before resuming activity.

If there is a problem with erection or ejaculation, it may be drug-related. Certain medications, especially those prescribed for high blood pressure, can interfere with sexual function. This should be brought to the attention of the physician, who may want to change the medication.

TRAVEL

Air or car travel is perfectly permissible if the treating physician agrees. Traveling on an airplane will not affect the heart; however, it is important for leg circulation to get up and walk around the plane every hour or so. Simple leg exercises such as flexing the knees, ankles, and toes are also helpful while sitting. A five-minute walk each hour during long car and plane trips is recommended to prevent pooling of blood in the extremities.

It is generally a good idea to carry important medications in the purse or pocket, and not pack them in a suitcase, to prevent losing or misplacing the medicine. The patient would be wise to ask the cardiologist or surgeon for the name of a doctor and hospital in the area to which he will be traveling in case an emergency should arise.

Weight

Some physicians suggest that their patients weigh themselves daily or every other day, preferably in the morning before breakfast. A sudden weight gain in excess of three or four pounds (if it is not due to an overindulgence of food the day before) may indicate that the body is retaining fluid as a result of too much salt in the diet or for any one of a number of reasons.

The effects of overweight on the heart have been discussed in this and previous chapters. If the cardiologist feels his patient is overweight, he may put him on a special diet or he may simply suggest cutting down on food intake. Regrettably, it is far easier to recognize the need to lose weight than to actually undertake a diet. Here are a dozen favorite tips on "how we do it" gathered from a special group of open heart patients:

—Eat only at a kitchen table or dining-room table, at a place that has been set with silverware and a plate.

—Try to eat three meals a day at fairly regular times.

—Don't skip a meal—that only makes you hungrier for the next one.

—Do not do anything else while you eat, such as reading or watching television.

—Whenever possible, try to have company during a meal. Keep the conversation light and the pace relaxed. Try to take at least twenty minutes to a half hour for each meal.

—Eat small portions. Don't keep serving plates on the table.

—Always shop for food from a list. Shop after you have eaten. Do not buy foods that are likely to be tempting or high in calories.

—Keep low-calorie snacks such as carrot sticks and celery in the refrigerator cleaned and ready to eat.

—Ask your family to help by not tempting you with edible things you love.

—Ask well-meaning friends not to visit with gifts of food.

—Plan ahead for special occasions by eating less at breakfast and lunch.

—*Never,* never, never adopt the "latest" fad diet. They don't work! (If they did, there would never be a need for the "latest" fad diet.)

When to Visit or Call the Doctor

Patients who live in the same locale as their heart surgeon will probably see him for at least one postoperative visit, but those who travel a long distance to a heart center may not return once the hospital stay is over. In general, patients are advised to see their family physician and/or cardiologist at some time within the first six weeks after the operation.

The physician should *always* be notified of any suspected problems, including the following:

—Chest pain or angina (not to be confused with pain in the chest wall that comes from the natural healing process).

—Shortness of breath that continues after an activity is stopped.

—Sudden weight gain.

—Unusually long periods of fatigue. Some fatigue can be expected, however, as the body's normal reaction to the recovery.

—Persistent fever lower than 100 degrees Fahrenheit for more than one week.

—Any fever higher than 100 degrees Fahrenheit.

—Swelling of the legs.

—Redness around any of the incisional areas.

It is important to use common sense in dealing with postoperative problems. Patients should not be afraid to call a doctor if problems exist or are suspected. Often the surgeon's nurse or assistant has been trained to answer questions that are common to recovering patients, and will be able to assess the situation and make the proper judgment in most instances.

Chapter Fourteen

Postoperative Complications

These are the things that happen to the other guy.
—VINCENT P., fifty-eight years old

O PEN HEART SURGERY PATIENTS have far fewer postoperative complications today than they had in the past. One reason is that new, sophisticated diagnostic techniques make preoperative patient evaluation more accurate. And because the number of patients being operated on is growing so fast, heart centers are developing a high level of expertise in the care of these patients. This is true not only of the physicians but of the nursing and paramedical personnel as well.

In spite of all reasonable precautions, however, problems can still arise. And although major complications are few, even *one* is too many. What are these complications? How can they be prevented? Who gets them? And why do some people seem to sail through surgery while others develop all kinds of problems?

An uncomplicated postoperative course is not just luck. Many factors play a role, probably the most important of which is the general health and life style of the patient before the operation. Patients who smoke, for example, are more likely to develop postoperative lung complications than those who do not, because a smoker's lungs do not return to normal as quickly after surgery as those of a nonsmoker. People who are extremely overweight may find it harder to move about in the early postoperative period, thus increasing the possibility of problems with the lungs and the circulation in the legs. And if a patient has had a previous heart attack he may be slower to recover from the operation because his heart is weaker going into it.

EARLY POSTOPERATIVE COMPLICATIONS

Most problems that develop after open heart surgery, if problems develop at all, occur within a day or two after the operation. Some can be remedied within a few days and others require prolonged observation and therapy after discharge from the hospital. Following are some of the more common postoperative complications:

Lung Complications

It is *imperative* to cough immediately after surgery, even though it is uncomfortable, because it helps prevent pneumonia. The lungs normally contain mucus and fluids in the tissues that protect them from the effects of any particles in the air that is taken in with each breath. But the fluids can only do their job if they are kept in motion. If allowed to settle, they can seriously interfere with the oxygen exchange. This is why patients must cough as much as they are able to and why they should turn from side to side in bed periodically. Additionally, if mucous plugs block the tiny bronchial tubes, bacteria can collect behind them. When the normal self-cleansing action of the lungs is inhibited, infection can occur.

Vascular Complications

A common vascular complication is phlebitis of the leg veins, which is generally the result of immobility. Lying in bed in the CCU causes the circulation to become sluggish, and the blood tends to pool in the leg veins. When venous blood circulation slows down, small clots may begin to form. The clots, called emboli when they become dislodged, move through the bloodstream and can end up in the lungs. This may lead to serious breathing problems, depending upon the size of the clot.

As a way of preventing such complications, physical therapy is usually started as early in the recovery process as the patient's condition will allow. Therapy is designed to prevent problems associated with bed rest and to relieve tension and anxiety.

One precautionary measure is the use of surgical stockings that put gentle pressure on the legs to discourage blood from pooling in the veins and to prevent clots from forming. Bending and straightening the ankles and toes help the circulation as well. Whenever possible, the legs, particularly the leg from which the saphenous vein has been removed, should be elevated to hip level when the patient sits.

Cardiac Arrhythmias

Cardiac arrhythmias (irregular heartbeats) occur in approximately a fifth of the patients who have had open heart surgery. Irregular heartbeats are a result of an upset in the electrical conduction system, which can occur during or after surgery. Heart rates that become too fast or too slow are usually easily controlled with medication or with an adjustment by an external temporary pacemaker. With constant monitoring of the EKG by the CCU staff, these arrhythmias are detected rapidly and can be treated appropriately.

Post-Cardiotomy Syndrome

The symptoms of post-cardiotomy syndrome, including fever and minor aches, usually occur within the first few weeks after surgery. Sometimes the manifestation of post-cardiotomy syndrome is chest pain.

There are many theories about what causes post-cardiotomy syndrome. Some physicians describe it as a reaction of the outer covering of the heart to the trauma of the surgery. Others feel it may be the result of an auto-immune response that takes place within the body during the healing process.

Patients often confuse chest pain from post-cardiotomy syndrome with anginal pain. Anginal pain is usually of short duration, is similar to the pain experienced before the operation, and is relieved by nitroglycerin, whereas prolonged pain is more likely to be due to other causes.

Any chest pain after the operation should be reported to the physician, who will be able to determine the precise cause of the pain after he has performed a thorough examination.

Postoperative Psychosis

Anesthesia administered during the operation is sometimes responsible for changes in the mental process early in the postoperative period. Until the effects of the anesthesia completely wear off, patients may feel a sense of fogginess and disorientation. A slight change in mental state may also be a result of the time spent on the heart-lung machine, or it may come from medicines, especially the sedatives and painkillers that the patient receives postoperatively. Because different people react differently to the same drugs, what is one man's painkiller can become another man's hallucinogen. If this happens, the physician will adjust the dosage of the medication or substitute another.

Postoperative psychosis may be caused by "sensory overload" or "sleep deprivation." Patients wake up in a strange environment (the CCU) with tubes and wires emerging from different parts of their bodies. Sleep rhythms are lost as the continuous bright lights make night indistinguishable from day; because sleeping patients are often disturbed for medicines or coughing exercises, a good night's sleep, for the first few days, is virtually impossible.

Postoperative psychosis appears to be less frequent in patients who know what to expect. This is why so many heart centers now include a patient educator as a member of the team.

Neurological Complications

Although occurring from a physical insult to the brain, neurological complications are sometimes hard to differentiate from postoperative psychosis. Despite the careful efforts by the surgeon to avoid them, it appears that a very small percentage of patients having heart surgery is affected with true neurological complications. Although technical problems during the operation at one time accounted for the majority of these complications, most of them now occur when small arteries to the brain that were previously narrowed by atherosclerotic plaques become blocked during the operation, thereby depriving the brain of oxygen. Depending on how severely the brain is affected, the result may be a stroke, paralysis, speech defects, or blindness. Occasionally neurological complications can result in a state of confusion or memory loss; but these generally are transient symptoms, meaning they will pass eventually.

Postoperative Bleeding

Excessive bleeding or hemorrhage can occur postoperatively if the clotting properties of the blood are significantly altered during the blood's passage through the heart-lung machine. Fortunately, this can usually be corrected by transfusing special blood products and other medications. When bleeding does not stop spontaneously, the surgeons may need to reopen the chest incision to be sure that a hole in a small blood vessel was not the cause of the problem. This reoperation does not substantially alter the postoperative course, and once the bleeding is controlled, the patient's recovery continues normally.

Perioperative Myocardial Infarction

A heart attack that occurs immediately before, during, or within several days after surgery is known as a "perioperative" infarction. It can occur as a result of several things, most notably the inability of the heart to tolerate the deprivation of blood during the operation. As was previously discussed, stopping the circulation to the heart is essential during the time surgery is performed directly on the heart. In most cases this does not cause a problem, since the period of time the heart is bloodless is kept to a minimum and well-monitored. Perioperative infarction occurs in less than

4 percent of patients. It is usually so mild that there are no symptoms and it can only be detected by tests taken routinely during the postoperative period. Such infarctions usually do not interfere with normal recovery.

LATE POSTOPERATIVE PROBLEMS

Post-Pump Syndrome

This is a common complication following discharge from the hospital. Symptoms that may occur any time up to three months after surgery are fever, chills, headache, or a general feeling of aches and pains. Post-pump syndrome is thought to be related to the body's reaction to being on the heart-lung machine. It generally runs its course quickly and there should be no cause for concern. But if symptoms persist for more than a few days the doctor should be notified, because certain medicines will alleviate the problem almost immediately.

Recurrence of Angina

It seems the one thing most feared by anyone undergoing bypass surgery is that his chest pain will return. Unfortunately, within ten years this does occur in approximately 15 percent of patients. A number of things can cause angina to return. One is what doctors call "incomplete revascularization," meaning there were an inadequate number of bypasses performed to supply the heart with the blood it needs to keep it free from pain. This can happen if the surgeon is unable to see or reach a desired coronary artery, or if the disease is so widespread that narrowings occur all the way to the tip of the artery, leaving no room to place the bypass graft. In some cases the artery is too small to attach a graft to it. The surgeon must also consider the amount of time that a patient has been on the heart-lung machine and the heart has been in a "bloodless" state; he may feel it is more important to return blood to the heart after three or four grafts have been placed than to continue to keep it ischemic (free from oxygen) in order to place another graft.

Another reason for the recurrence of angina is a shut-down of the bypass graft. There is a 10 percent rate of closure within ten years for each graft. But this does not mean that if one graft closes they all close. Actually, one graft may close and the rest may remain open for life. Most often, grafts close because the recipient coronary artery was very tiny in the first place or the disease simply progressed beyond the graft.

The chief cause for returning chest pain is progression of existing coronary artery disease in ungrafted arteries. It has been mentioned before that bypass surgery does not cure coronary artery disease. It merely bypasses the existing narrowings or blockages in the artery. The disease continues to progress as time goes on, with the rate of progression being determined by the number of risk factors still present. Progressive disease is most common in patients who do not stop smoking.

Many people ask if disease develops in the new grafts. The answer to that is "sometimes." But the progression of new disease in the graft itself is very slow, and in general takes years to build up to the point of significantly narrowing it. Therefore, it is safe to say that with the normal rate of progression of atherosclerosis, the chances are that the new bypass grafts will *not* develop enough plaque to make any significant difference to the functioning of the heart. In other words, the new graft will probably outlive the patient.

Late Valve Complications

If a problem arises in patients who have had valve replacements, it is often related to the bleeding from anticoagulant medications they are taking. Mechanical valves require anticoagulants to prevent the tendency for clots to develop around them. Although most metal valves last a lifetime, there is always a small possibility, as with all mechanical things, of functional defects developing over the course of many years. Tissue valves usually require no anticoagulants but do have a higher rate of failure within ten to fifteen years and may need to be replaced at some time.

Since body chemistry is constantly changing, the dosage of anticoagulant medication must be monitored by a blood test about once a month. If there is inadequate anticoagulant in the blood, small clots may develop on the valve; the clots can travel to any part of the body and become lodged in a crucial area, causing serious problems. On the other hand, if there is too much anticoagulant, spontaneous bleeding may occur in the stomach, skin, or brain. Therefore, continued supervision by the physician is essential.

Incisional Problems

One minor problem, but not really a complication, is worth mentioning because it is fairly common. For the six to nine months it takes for the breastbone to heal completely, aching or itching may occur in the area of the chest incision when the weather changes or it is going to rain. In fact, it is often said that no matter how sophisticated the equipment for forecasting weather, nothing is more accurate than a patient who has had a recent chest incision.

Incisional pain like this can be alleviated with a mild pain reliever. It is best, however, to check with a physician before taking any medication other than that which has been previously prescribed.

Chapter Fifteen

What's New: A Brief Look Ahead

Sure—they have their new hearts of plastic and steel.
And that's fine . . . But for my money, the original
can never be equaled!

—ROSS T., sixty-two years old

THE ASTOUNDING ADVANCES in the treatment of heart disease since its beginning have been charted in the previous chapters. The most encouraging statistic is that during the past decade the death rate from heart disease in the United States has plummeted by 25 percent.

There is a variety of reasons for this: better emergency care, improved diagnostic and surgical techniques, and new drug therapies. Probably the greatest factor, however, is the increased public awareness of the causes and prevention of heart disease. More people are having annual checkups, smoking has declined, there is a greater recognition of the importance of treating high blood pressure, and there have been dramatic changes in the American diet. For example, in this country from 1950 to 1978, the consumption of eggs and dairy fats fell about 30 percent, and the consumption of animal fats fell about 80 percent. Americans are exercising more and are more conscious of fitness and health. Today people who have heart disease have available to them an array of technology that did not exist twenty-five years ago. The heart-lung machine, nuclear scanning devices, electronic defibrillators, mobile emergency care units, pacemakers, heart valves, and even the availability of blood pressure machines in local supermarkets have all been factors in the death rate's downward trend.

NEWER DIAGNOSTIC TECHNIQUES

For many patients with coronary heart disease the first "symptom" is sudden death; about 300,000 patients die suddenly each year. Consequently, it has become extremely important to develop screening procedures to alert the physician to the presence of the disease *before* symptoms occur.

One exciting method of evaluating the coronary arteries is now being perfected. A noninvasive test called digital subtraction angiography can disclose the existence and extent of atherosclerosis without the need for inserting a catheter into the body. Because the test can be done without hospitalization, it is much less expensive than a standard arteriogram. A small amount of dye injected into a vein travels through the bloodstream. A computer that has been programmed to select a specific area for study produces a composite image of the heart or blood vessels much like an x-ray but with enhanced quality and detail.

This technique is now being used successfully to demonstrate narrowing of the larger arteries of the neck and abdomen. There is hope that soon it will be extended to the coronary arteries, but at the moment the images from digital angiography are not clear enough to define the exact anatomy of the coronaries. Consequently, a standard coronary arteriogram is still required for the "operative road map" of where to place the bypasses. It may only be a matter of time, however, before the new noninvasive technique becomes accurate enough to replace standard catheterization.

NEWER DRUG THERAPIES

In addition to improvements in defining the anatomy and refinements in surgical technique, medical therapy is also changing. New drugs are constantly being developed, as well as new uses for existing drugs. The front runners are the beta-blockers, which were introduced in this country in the 1970s and are now widely prescribed for various heart problems. These drugs block the action of the beta receptors, the nerves that affect the heart rate and force of contraction. Beta-blockers, the most common of which is propranolol (Inderal), were first used to treat arrhythmias. Now, however, their use has been expanded to include treatment of angina and high blood pressure. And the most exciting news is that the drugs have proven to be effective in preventing second heart attacks and sudden death. A government study of 3,837 patients showed a reduced mortality of 26 percent in heart attack survivors who were subsequently treated with propranolol.

Added to this group of "miracle workers" is a new class of agents known as the calcium, or slow-channel, blockers. These drugs, such as nifedipine and verapamil, interfere with calcium ions, the chemical that makes muscles contract, and therefore allow the coronary arteries to expand and ultimately to carry more blood to the heart. And since the heart will pump less forcefully because it is deprived of calcium, these drugs greatly reduce arrhythmias and allow the heart afflicted by a heart attack to rest and rebuild its damaged tissue.

HEART TRANSPLANTS

It has been fifteen years since the world's first heart transplant took place. Although the event initially showed spectacular promise, the survival rates of the recipients proved disappointing. In fact, many centers that had begun transplant programs in the early 1970s eventually chose to discontinue them. But now there is a new drug available called Cyclosporin A, which has reduced the frequency and severity of rejection of the transplant and secondarily reduced the frequency of infection.

Before Cyclosporin A became available, patients were given huge doses of immunosuppressant drugs to prevent rejection of the foreign tissue of their new heart. But these powerful antirejection drugs so altered the normal immune system that the patient was left with no resistance to infection. Most patients died of infection, not from rejection of the new heart. Cyclosporin A acts to inhibit the cells that cause rejection but does not interfere with those that fight infection. Although use of this drug is in its early stages, preliminary patient survival rates have improved enough to generate renewed interest in heart transplants throughout the country.

PERMANENT ARTIFICIAL HEARTS

After many years of research and preparation, a permanent artificial heart was recently implanted into the chest of the first human recipient. Although the mechanics of the heart require the patient to be continuously connected to a cumbersome machine, researchers are working on a future version that will ultimately provide power for the heart in the form of a five-pound battery pack that can be strapped to the patient's waist. This astounding advance in cardiac technology has offered new hope to those who, for some reason, cannot receive a heart transplant.

NEWER NONSURGICAL TECHNIQUES

A heart attack occurs when a coronary artery suddenly becomes completely occluded after gradually having become narrowed over a period of years. The final obstruction is usually due to a blood clot. If the patient can be brought to the hospital within a few hours of the attack, there is a chance that this "lethal" clot can be dissolved by injecting a clot-dissolving substance directly into the coronary artery. Enzymes called thrombolysins are injected through a special catheter in order to dissolve the clot and reestablish the blood flow that existed before the clot formed. This technique, known as coronary thrombolysis, is only a stop-gap measure to prevent or reverse the muscle damage of the heart attack. In some cases bypass surgery is still needed after thrombolysis because the original narrowing of the artery could not be dissolved.

Another new technique, known as percutaneous transluminal coronary angioplasty (PTCA) or "balloon angioplasty," was introduced in the United States in 1977 by Dr. Andreas Gruntzig of Zurich, Switzerland. This procedure dilates the coronary arteries at the point where they have become narrowed by plaque. A special catheter with a tiny deflated balloon at its tip is passed through an artery in the arm or leg into the coronary artery to the point where it is centered within the narrowed area. The balloon is then inflated to compress the plaque against the arterial wall and widen the narrowing. When the catheter is withdrawn, the plaque remains compressed and blood flow through the artery is improved.

This procedure is most successful in patients with a localized obstruction of just one or two arteries. If PTCA is unsuccessful, at times it may be necessary to perform an immediate coronary bypass operation. Physicians and researchers are anxiously awaiting the long-term results of this technique, which may be an important alternative to coronary bypass surgery.

ARRHYTHMIA STUDY

Electrophysiology, a new subspecialty in the field of cardiology, is the study of disorders of the heartbeat and of the heart's conduction system. The goal of the study is to determine what type of disorder exists and to identify the specific area or pathways that give rise to the abnormal rhythm. Electrodes threaded into the heart are used to study the electrocardiogram from within its chambers, and to induce rhythmic disturbances so that the characteristics can be studied more closely to evaluate various drugs or pacing techniques. Once the doctor knows what kind of disorder is present, he can prescribe the proper treatment. Sometimes treatment may even involve removal of the focus of the arrhythmia through open heart surgery.

STATUS OF CORONARY BYPASS SURGERY

During the early 1980s, with coronary bypass surgery becoming almost as routine as gallbladder surgery, heart specialists turned their attention to one major question: Can the coronary artery bypass operation stand the test of time in not only improving the quality of life but also extending life? It is now clear that the answer to this question is an emphatic "Yes." Not only will a successful coronary artery bypass operation restore the patient to a pain-free state at least 90 percent of the time, but statistics show that in many cases the patient will live longer than if he had not undergone the operation.

MEDICINE VERSUS SURGERY DEBATE

As new drugs and safe surgery have become available almost simultaneously, the important question every cardiologist and patient faces is: Which mode of therapy is most appropriate for the patient's particular condition? The news media have occasionally whipped up this debate by reporting new techniques without carefully identifying the subgroup of patients who would benefit from it. Consequently, whenever a new technique is announced many heart patients feel that it should be used in their case without fully understanding whether or not it would be helpful.

In the past, cardiologists and surgeons often disagreed on the appropriate way to manage a patient's heart disease. Because cardiologists tend to be experts on drug therapy or noninvasive treatment, and heart surgeons tend to be experts on operative therapy, each would favor his own area of expertise. Today the decision whether or not to operate is less subjective. For example, in valvular disease or congenital heart defects, the decision is not so much *whether* to operate as *when* to operate. A more problematic issue, however, concerns patients with coronary artery disease. Coronary bypass surgery had been so controversial that the National Heart, Lung and Blood Institute felt compelled to conduct an investigative study of its status in this country. The report, issued in 1981, contained this question: "What is the overall management of coronary artery disease; that is, in what context should coronary artery surgery be considered?" A summary of the answer is as follows:

If the final medical workup indicates that the patient is at high risk of sudden death or a heart attack—for example, if the patient has severe narrowing of the left main coronary artery or severe narrowing of multiple major coronary branches—surgery is given especially serious consideration. If, on the other hand, the studies indicate no critical narrowing of any major coronary branch, surgery is clearly not indicated and medical treatment is advised.

The next question then becomes: What should be done about the large number of patients who fall between these extremes? In these patients, recommendations are based upon two fundamental considerations. The first issue is to determine which course will provide the greatest protection from a heart attack or sudden death. That is to say, is there sufficient narrowing of one or more arteries to jeopardize the viability of a considerable segment of heart muscle? If so, the operation would be suggested to preserve the muscle. The second issue is to choose the course that will permit a satisfactory quality of life according to the patient's own standards. These decisions are highly subjective. One is based largely upon the physician's interpretation of the data. The second depends upon the way the individual responds to medical therapy and on his own appraisal of the extent of his disability and restrictions.

It is universal practice for the physician, when faced with this problem, to institute medical therapy and periodically to reevaluate the patient's response. This approach requires careful education of the patient and spouse on the nature of the disease and its management to permit adequate self-care and to allow the patient to participate knowledgeably in major decisions affecting his life. It requires control of risk factors for atherosclerosis and modification of life style in both work and leisure activities. It may require long-term administration of such potent medications as nitroglycerin, beta-blockers, long-acting nitrites, antiarrhythmic agents, and digitalis. If, after such careful and intensive medical treatment, the patient finds that the quality of his life is still unsatisfactory, he must then seek alternative treatment and surgery may be advised.

Advances in cardiology over the last decade have come at a lightning pace compared to the years before. New achievements are recorded almost daily. Still the war against heart disease continues, with the spectacular successes only serving to make new challenges worth pursuing. For progress, it seems, comes not in knowing all the answers but in realizing how many questions still remain.

Chapter Sixteen

Frequently Asked Questions About Heart Surgery

With Answers by Mark S. Hochberg, M.D.

Why do I need heart surgery to fix my heart when my co-worker's heart was fixed with just a pacemaker?

Your heart operation was or will be performed because of either coronary artery disease or valvular heart disease. A pacemaker is designed to help a problem that is entirely different: an abnormal heart rhythm, the beating pattern of the heart.

I am afraid I will not be fully asleep during the operation. Does that ever happen?

No. Anesthesia during heart surgery is provided by doctors who usually deal only with cardiac patients. Vivid dreams following surgery may sometimes be mistaken for remembered real events, but I do not know of a single instance of an individual who postoperatively could relate any events that occurred during the operation.

How many bypasses can I have?

A patient can have up to six or seven bypasses, the risk of which is not all that different from one or two. Your surgeon will do as many bypasses as he feels you need following evaluation of your arteriogram and your heart.

Is it true that the more bypasses you have, the better off you are?
No. You need to have all significant narrowings or obstructions bypassed if technically possible. The reasons for doing or not doing a bypass are complex. Perhaps you only have disease in one vessel and the rest of your heart is normal. On the other hand, you may have many diseased vessels but only one large enough to take a bypass. In these two instances, only one bypass would be done, but the long-term results could be very different.

Two years ago I had my varicose saphenous veins removed. Now what will they use for my bypasses?
This is one of the most frustrating problems for heart surgeons. Fortunately you have other veins that never become varicosed. These veins lie in the back of the calves and were not removed at the time of your original vein operation. In addition, the internal mammary artery, which lies just below the breastbone, can be used as a conduit for bypass grafting. On rare occasions synthetic arteries may be used. To my knowledge no individual has ever been turned down for heart surgery because of lack of veins.

Will I need private nurses?
No. The most critical time following the heart operation is in the coronary care unit. Here specially trained nursing personnel deliver the expert care you need, and there are usually no more than two patients assigned to each nurse. You will not be transferred from the coronary care unit until you are no longer in need of private nursing care.

Why is my roommate progressing so much faster than I am?
As you probably realize, the extent of heart disease varies from individual to individual. In part, your rate of recovery will depend on how quickly your heart can return to normal. For example, someone who has had no heart attacks prior to surgery obviously will improve more rapidly than someone who has had several. Another consideration is your overall physical status going into the operation. Patients who are very sick before surgery are sometimes slower to recover than those who are in better physical health.

Why do people run a fever after the operation?
It is not necessarily because you have an infection. Everyone runs a fever for the first day or two after an operation as part of the body's reaction to the stress of surgery. Another reason not due to infection is the lack of full use of your lungs. Specifically, when you have a chest incision, it is difficult to take deep breaths and cough. When the lungs are not completely expanded, the small airways collapse, causing a condition known as atelectasis, which is accompanied by fever. However, there are ways to improve your ability to breathe deeply. By taking deep breaths and coughing, the small air spaces expand and the sputum can be freed and coughed up. Once you get into the swing of coughing and deep breathing, the fever usually disappears.

Are painkilling medicines addictive?
Many patients shy away from asking for morphine or Demerol during the immediate postoperative period because they are afraid that they will become addicted to it.

This cannot happen given the small amounts of the drugs used and the number of days their use is required. Usually the most severe pain occurs only within the first few days following your operation. The important thing is not to be a "hero." Painkillers are given so you can do the deep breathing and coughing that are required to prevent atelectasis. On the other hand, it is important not to take too much pain medication and make yourself constantly sleepy for several days. Rather you might try to determine how much medication you need so you can stay fully alert and yet minimize the discomfort of the operation.

I just had bypass surgery. Is my heart disease cured?

In a narrow sense the operation does not cure coronary atherosclerosis. The significant narrowings that you have will continue to get worse and completely occlude the vessel(s). However, the bypass permits the blood to flow around and beyond the blockage so the effects of the complete obstruction of the vessel by atherosclerosis will not be felt and further damage to the heart may well be prevented. So, although there is nothing that is done for the atherosclerosis, the operation does protect against its damage. Over the ensuing years, new cholesterol plaques or deposits can occur in other vessels. However, this usually happens very gradually, taking many years to become significant.

If my heart is fixed, why must I change my life style?

The goal of the operation is to return you to a better life style than you had just prior to the operation. The usual circumstance before surgery is that an individual is limited from doing his job or taking part in athletics because of chest pain. After successful surgery, most people are able to perform these tasks without the chest pain or discomfort that existed in the preoperative period. So there really needs to be no change in your work or athletic habits from before the operation. The important modification is to eliminate risk factors that might speed up your coronary artery disease. Specifically, you should try to maintain a normal weight and to stop smoking.

Will the bypass grafts clog up just like the coronary arteries did?
There is a very small possibility that the coronary bypasses will develop atherosclerosis similar to that in the coronary arteries. In fact, the chance of this happening to a significant degree is less than 5 percent. If this occurs and chest pain recurs, then additional bypasses can be performed. However, in general it is not a major problem. As stated earlier, it has taken you many years to develop significant disease in your coronary arteries. It is hoped that it would take you at least the same number of years to develop similar degrees of narrowing in your coronary bypasses.

What are your recommendations for the immediate period following discharge from the hospital?
The single most important aspect of postoperative care at home is daily exercise. You may want to get into a self-help or professional rehabilitation program following your heart surgery. This involves daily physical activity such as walking, swimming, golf, bicycling, etc. The worst thing you can do is to be sedentary all week and then exercise on a weekend. It is wise to work yourself back into shape much as an athlete does in spring training.

From day one following discharge from the hospital, you should be doing daily exercise. Initially this usually means walking. If the weather is cold or inclement, shopping malls provide perfect places to walk and rest. Everyone progresses at a different rate of speed, but I tell my patients that by three or four weeks after operation they should walk two to three miles *every single day*.

What diet should I follow after heart surgery?
It is important to regain your full strength and to do what is best for your heart. An initial concern is to avoid excess salt. For the first several weeks at home you should avoid table salt and heavily salted foods such as potato chips, pretzels, pizza, etc. Once you are back to fairly normal status, you should check with your cardiologist about the proper amount of salt.

The question of high, low, or minimal cholesterol diets is always uppermost in a patient's mind. At present, we are gathering evidence regarding the effects of cholesterol on people with and without heart disease. Many studies are now under way to determine if the cholesterol and fat intake following heart surgery will affect its ultimate success. However, the data on this subject are not yet conclusive and therefore you should follow the dietary advice of your cardiologist.

If I can ride in a car for the first six weeks following the operation, why can't I drive one?
There are really two important reasons for the restriction against driving for six weeks after operation. The first reason is that your sternum, or breastbone, is healing much like any other broken bone. Stopping short and

forcing your chest against a steering wheel could injure the healing breastbone. In addition, driving a car is far more stressful an activity than you might realize. This stress should be eliminated during the immediate postoperative period.

When may I return to work?

Motivation is critical to returning to work. One patient of mine returned to coaching his Little League team only nine days following his coronary bypass operation. Another patient returned to his job as a high school guidance counselor twelve days following his heart operation. Needless to say, both of these individuals returned to these pursuits against my advice! As with an athlete returning to full activity, it is important to set goals for yourself.

In general, a good-risk patient with a reasonably normal heart can expect to return part-time to his desk job four to six weeks following heart surgery. Usually one can begin doing office paperwork at home on a very limited basis one to two weeks following hospital discharge (three to four weeks following actual date of operation). However, a job requiring heavy manual labor might require up to six months for complete rehabilitation. Returning to work is something you need to discuss with your cardiologist and heart surgeon. I would anticipate that every individual who wants to do so can return to work following heart surgery.

APPENDICES

Patient Resources

Many organizations around the country offer professional guidance, public information, and personal support to people concerned about heart disease and heart surgery. Listed below are some of these organizations and their addresses. Also listed are publications available at minimal or no charge that offer information directly concerned with specific aspects of heart disease or heart surgery.

PROFESSIONAL ORGANIZATIONS

American Association for
    Thoracic Surgery
6 Beacon Street
Boston, MA 02108

American Board of Thoracic
    Surgery
1405 East Ann Street
P.O. Box 32
Ann Arbor, MI 48109

American College of
    Cardiology
9111 Old Georgetown Road
Bethesda, MD 20014

American College of
    Surgeons
55 East Erie Street
Chicago, IL 60611

American Hospital
    Association
840 North Lakeshore Drive
Chicago, IL 60611

American Medical
    Association
535 North Dearborn Street
Chicago, IL 60611

American Nurses Association
2420 Pershing Road
Kansas City, MO 64108

Association of American
  Physicians and Surgeons
2111 Enco Drive
Suite N 515–519
Oak Brook, IL 60521

International Cardiovascular
  Society
5323 Harry Hines Boulevard
Dallas, TX 75235

Society for Thoracic Surgery
111 East Wacker Drive
Chicago, IL 60601

Society for Vascular Surgery
c/o Department of Surgery
UCLA School of Medicine
Center for the Health Sciences
Los Angeles, CA 90024

GOVERNMENT ORGANIZATIONS

The National Institutes of Health (NIH)
Bethesda, MD 20205

The National Heart, Lung and Blood Institute
Bethesda, MD 20014

AMERICAN HEART ASSOCIATION

Organized in 1942, the American Heart Association (AHA) is a voluntary nonprofit organization extensively involved in research, service, and education. Information regarding the type of services available in specific localities may be obtained from the AHA local units, chartered divisions, or the national headquarters at 7320 Greenville Avenue, Dallas, TX 75231.

Listed below are state divisions, which may be contacted directly.

Alabama Affiliate
1449 Medical Park Drive
Birmingham, AL 35213

Alaska Heart Association
2330 East 42nd Street
Anchorage, AK 99504

Arizona Affiliate
1445 East Thomas
Phoenix, AZ 85014

Arkansas Affiliate
909 West 2nd Street
Little Rock, AR 72201

California Affiliate
805 Burlway Road
Burlingame, CA 94010

Greater Los Angeles Affiliate
2405 West 8th Street
Los Angeles, CA 90057

Colorado Heart Association
4521 East Virginia Avenue
Denver, CO 80222

Connecticut Affiliate, Inc.
71 Parker Avenue
Meriden, CT 06450

Dakota Affiliate
1005 Twelfth Avenue, S.E.
Jamestown, ND 58401

American Heart Association
of Delaware, Inc.
4C Trolley Square
Delaware Avenue and
  Dupont Street
Wilmington, DE 19806

District of Columbia
(See Nation's Capital)

Florida Affiliate
810 63rd Avenue North
St. Petersburg, FL 33702

Georgia Affiliate
Level C, Broadway Plaza
2581 Piedmont Road, N.E.
Atlanta, GA 30324

American Heart Association
of Hawaii, Inc.
245 North Kukui Street
Honolulu, HI 96817

Idaho Affiliate
5777 Overland Road
Boise, ID 83705

Illinois Affiliate, Inc.
1181 North Dirksen Parkway
Springfield, IL 62708

Chicago Heart Association
20 North Wacker Drive
Chicago, IL 60606

Indiana Affiliate, Inc.
222 South Downey, Suite 222
Indianapolis, IN 46219

Iowa Affiliate
1111 Office Park Road
West Des Moines, IA 50254

Kansas Affiliate
5229 West 7th Street
Topeka, KS 66606

Kentucky Affiliate, Inc.
207 Speed Building
Louisville, KY 40202

Louisiana Affiliate, Inc.
3303 Tulane Avenue
New Orleans, LA 70119

Maine Affiliate, Inc.
20 Winter Street
Augusta, ME 04330

Maryland Affiliate, Inc.
425 North Charles Street
Baltimore, MD 21203

Massachusetts Affiliate, Inc.
33 Broad Street
Boston, MA 02109

Michigan Heart Association
16310 West Twelve Mile
    Road
Lathrup Village, MI 48076

Minnesota Affiliate, Inc.
4701 West 77th Street
Minneapolis, MN 55435

Mississippi Affiliate
4830 East Willie Circle
Jackson, MS 39206

Missouri Affiliate
105 East Ash, Suite 2
Columbia, MO 65201

Montana Heart Association
Professional Building
510 1st Avenue, North
Great Falls, MT 59401

Nation's Capital Affiliate
2233 Wisconsin Avenue,
    N.W.
Washington, DC 20007

Nebraska Affiliate
3624 Farnam
Omaha, NB 68131

Nevada Affiliate
805 Burlway Road
Burlingame, CA 94010

New Hampshire Heart
    Association
2 Industrial Park Drive
Concord, NH 03301

New Jersey Affiliate
1525 Morris Avenue
Union, NJ 07083

New Mexico Affiliate
2403 San Mateo, N.E., Suite
    W-14
Albuquerque, NM 87110

New York State Affiliate
214 South Warren Street, 8th
    Floor
Syracuse, NY 13202

New York Heart
Association, Inc.
205 East 42nd Street
New York, NY 10017

North Carolina Affiliate
One Heart Circle
Chapel Hill, NC 27514

Northeast Ohio Affiliate
1689 East 115th Street
Cleveland, OH 44106

Ohio Affiliate, Inc.
6161 Busch Boulevard, Suite
327
Columbus, OH 43229

Oklahoma Affiliate, Inc.
800 Northwest 15th Street
Oklahoma City, OK 73104

Oregon Affiliate
1500 S.W. 12th Avenue
Portland, OR 97201

Pennsylvania Affiliate
2743 North Front Street
Harrisburg, PA 17110

Puerto Rico Heart
Association
554 Cabo Alverio Street
Apartado Postal 1753
Hato Rey Station
San Juan, PR 00919

Rhode Island Affiliate, Inc.
40 Broad Street
Pawtucket, RI 02860

South Carolina Affiliate
5868 Percival Road
Columbia, SC 29260

Tennessee Affiliate
101 23rd Avenue, North
Nashville, TN 37203

Texas Affiliate, Inc.
860 East Anderson Lane
Austin, TX 78761

Utah Heart Association
250 East 1st South
Salt Lake City, UT 84111

Vermont Heart Association
R.D. #2, Box 2821
Shelburne, VT 05482

Virginia Affiliate, Inc.
316 East Clay Street
Richmond, VA 23219

American Heart Association
of Washington
4414 Woodland Park Avenue
North
Seattle, WA 98103

West Virginia Affiliate
211 35th Street, S.E.
Charleston, WV 25304

Wisconsin Affiliate, Inc.
795 North Van Buren Street
Milwaukee, WI 53202

American Heart Association
of Wyoming, Inc.
2015 Central Avenue
Cheyenne, WY 82001

LAY ORGANIZATIONS

Mended Hearts

The Mended Hearts, Inc., is an organization composed of people who have undergone open heart surgery. This nonprofit service group has over one hundred chapters across the country and a membership of 15,000 people.

The motto of the organization is "It's great to be alive and to help others." Specially trained members of the Mended Hearts visit patients in the hospital before or soon after heart surgery. Just seeing someone who is living proof of the success of the operation often gives patients and their families that extra bit of encouragement they need to get them through a difficult period. Anyone may become a member of the Mended Hearts. Active members are those who have had heart surgery and associate members are those who are interested in the group's purpose, but have not had the operation. A list of local chapters may be obtained by writing to:

The Mended Hearts, Inc.
7320 Greenville Avenue
Dallas, TX 75231

Zipper Club

With a philosophy very much like the Mended Hearts, Zipper Club members visit hospitalized open heart surgery patients in an effort to offer reassurance, information, or assistance. A list of local chapters may be obtained by contacting:

The Zipper Club
318 South 19th Street
Philadelphia, PA 19103

Weight Watchers

This organization has a longstanding reputation for successfully helping people to change their eating habits and to adopt
a way of life that includes a well-rounded diet, nutritionally
balanced and designed to help people lose weight. Weight
Watchers groups are in almost every city in the country. Listed
below is the address and telephone number of the national organization, which may be contacted for information regarding local
chapters. (It is advisable to check with your physician before
going on *any* diet.)

Weight Watchers International
800 Community Drive
Manhasset, NY 11030

Overeaters Anonymous

The program is run with a format similar to that of Alcoholics
Anonymous. Group support is offered to people who have here-
tofore had difficulty losing weight. Suggested diets vary from
group to group but the philosophy of people helping people
remains the same all over the country. Overeaters Anonymous
groups are listed in the telephone book.

Smokenders

This program was designed and is sponsored by the American
Cancer Society. Smokenders uses behavior modification and fac-
tual information to help people gradually discontinue the smoking habit. Programs are held periodically and may be located by
calling a local chapter of the American Cancer Society.

American Cancer Society
777 3rd Avenue
New York, NY 10017

INFORMATIVE MATERIALS

Listed below are materials made available to the public free of charge through the American Heart Association. Single copies may be ordered by writing to a local chapter of the AHA or to the National Headquarters at:

American Heart Association
7320 Greenville Avenue
Dallas, TX 75231

Heart Facts—1980
Published annually by the American Heart Association; reflects the latest information available on cardiovascular disease. Gives an explanation of the programs and the functions of the American Heart Association.

Five Facts You Should Know About Heart Disease
Easy-to-read leaflet; gives five hopeful facts about heart disease.

Heart and Blood Vessels
Illustrated booklet containing questions and answers regarding a healthy heart; coronary artery disease; stroke, high blood pressure, and other heart-related diseases.

Heart Attack
Easy-to-read explanation of a heart attack, angina pectoris, and coronary atherosclerosis. Gives some general rules for heart patients and what to do in case of a heart attack.

Heart Quiz
General information in question-and-answer form on facts most people want to know about heart disease.

High Blood Pressure
Easy-to-read leaflet answers the most asked questions regarding high blood pressure: what it is, what it does, diagnosis, and treatment.

High Blood Pressure and How to Control It
Explains what high blood pressure is, what it does to your body, how to find out if you have it, and what to do about it.

Living with Your Pacemaker
Explains the purpose and function of the device in simple terms and instructs the patient in self-care. Includes a page for individualized medical instruction and a tear-out emergency identification card.

E Is for Exercise
Explains role of exercise in heart health. Describes types of exercise recommended for cardiovascular fitness. Lists factors to be considered before beginning an exercise program.

Eat Well But Eat Wisely to Reduce Your Risk of Heart Attack
Nutrition leaflet with advice on reducing the risk of heart attack through diet modification.

Guide for Weight Reduction
Outlines three eating patterns at different calorie levels, plus helpful hints on how to select and prepare food.

Nutrition Labeling—Food Selection Hints for Fat-Controlling Meals
To assist the consumer in the selection of foods low in saturated fat and cholesterol for preparation of fat-controlled meals.

Recipes for Fat-Controlled, Low-Cholesterol Meals
Contains recipes for a fat-controlled, low-cholesterol diet.

Save Food and Help Your Heart
How to shop economically while selecting healthful foods. Contains hints on storing and preparing food.

Way to a Man's Heart, a Fat-Controlled, Low-Cholesterol Meal Plan to Reduce the Risk of Heart Attack
Explains the relationship of diet to heart disease. Shows how to select foods for a balanced diet low in saturated fat and cholesterol. Also lists the five basic food groups.

Weight Control Guidance in Smoking Cessation
For individuals on a smoking cessation program who are experiencing a weight gain. Discusses suggestions for weight maintenance or reduction.

How to Stop Smoking
Gives the reader an easy-to-follow five-step withdrawal program on how to stop smoking.

Older Person's Guide to Cardiovascular Health
Written with the senior citizen in mind. Suggests how to improve the quality of life as a person grows older. Presents information regarding cardiovascular diseases. Also gives a number of tips on planning a heart-healthy life style.

Reduce Your Risk of Heart Attack
Explains the major risks in heart attack and what you can do about them. With helpful facts about heart and circulation and atherosclerosis (artery disease) that underlies most heart attacks and strokes.

Take Care of Your Heart
Easy-to-read illustrated booklet. Gives the early warning signals of heart attack. Helpful for the individual suffering from hypertension and overweight.

The following U.S. government publications are available, free of charge, by writing to:

Publications Section
Public Inquiries and Reports Branch
National Heart, Lung and Blood Institute
Bethesda, MD 20205

How Doctors Diagnose Heart Disease
Describes the methods your doctor may employ in diagnosing heart or blood vessel disease.

The Human Heart—A Living Pump
Describes how the heart functions as a pump for the body's blood. Contains diagrams of the heart in action and the body's blood supply system. Also defines several basic heart terms.

Medicine for the Layman: Heart Attacks
Discusses heart attacks: what causes them, their symptoms, and where to go for help. Also presents information on how to help prevent heart attacks.

Fact Sheet: Arteriosclerosis
Presents in detail many aspects of the problem of arteriosclerosis: what it is, its consequences, magnitude, risk factors, research, and prevention.

Fact Sheet: Diabetes and Cardiovascular Disease
Defines and explains cardiovascular disease and diabetes and the relationship between them. Also briefly describes research being supported by the National Heart, Lung and Blood Institute on diabetes and cardiovascular disease. Provides suggestions for changes in life style that may be helpful to the diabetic.

Fact Sheet: Venous Thrombosis and Pulmonary Embolism
Describes venous thrombosis, factors affecting susceptibility to this condition, its diagnosis and treatment.

High Blood Pressure and What You Can Do About It
Describes the serious nature of high blood pressure, myths and facts about the disease, drugs used, and suggestions for staying with therapy.

High Blood Pressure Facts and Fiction
Presents facts to correct four major misconceptions about high blood pressure.

Questions About Weight, Salt, and High Blood Pressure
Describes what we know now about the relationship between diet changes and high blood pressure.

Suggested Reading

Alpert, Joseph S., *The Heart Attack Handbook: A Commonsense Guide to Treatment, Recovery, and Staying Well.* Boston: Little, Brown, 1978.

American Heart Association, *The American Heart Association Cookbook,* 3rd rev. ed. New York: McKay, 1979.

American Heart Association, *Heartbook: A Guide to Prevention and Treatment of Cardiovascular Diseases.* New York: Dutton, 1980.

Benson, Herbert, *The Relaxation Response.* New York: Morrow, 1975.

Brody, Jane, *Jane Brody's Nutrition Book: A Lifetime Guide to Good Eating for Better Health and Weight Control.* New York: Norton, 1981.

Cousins, Norman, *Anatomy of an Illness.* New York: Norton, 1979.

DeBakey, Michael, and Anthony Gotto, *The Living Heart.* New York: McKay, 1977.

Eckstein, Gustav, *The Body Has a Head.* New York: Harper and Row, 1969.

Franklin, Marshall, Martin Krauthamer, A. Razzak Tai, and Ann Pinchot, *The Heart Doctors' Heart Book.* New York: Bantam, 1976.

Friedman, Meyer, and Ray H. Rosenman, *Type A Behavior and Your Heart.* New York: Knopf, 1974.

Hawthorne, Peter, *The Transplanted Heart.* Chicago: Rand McNally, 1968.

Lear, Martha W., *Heartsounds.* New York: Simon & Schuster, 1980.

Likoff, William, Bernard Segal, and Lawrence Galton, *Your Heart.* Philadelphia: Lippincott, 1972.

Miller, Donald W., *The Practice of Coronary Artery Bypass Surgery.* New York: Plenum, 1977.

Miller, Jonathan, *The Body in Question.* New York: Random House, 1978.

Nierenberg, Judith, and Florence Janovic. *The Hospital Experience: A Complete Guide to Understanding and Participating in Your Own Care.* Indianapolis: Bobbs-Merrill, 1978.

Nolen, William A., *Surgeon Under the Knife.* New York: Coward, McCann and Geoghegan, 1976.

Poole, Victoria, *Thursday's Child.* Boston: Little, Brown, 1980.

Rayner, Claire, *Everything Your Doctor Would Tell You If He Had the Time.* New York: Putnam, 1981.

Thompson, Thomas, *Hearts: Of Surgeons and Transplants, Miracles and Disasters Along the Cardiac Frontier.* New York: McCall, 1971.

Glossary of
Medical Terms*

ANEURYSM   A spindle-shaped or saclike bulging of the wall of
a vein or artery, due to weakening of the wall by disease or an
abnormality present at birth. A ventricular aneurysm (usually
resulting from a heart attack) is a ballooning out in the wall of
the left ventricle to create a noncontractile sac.

ANGINA   A condition in which the heart muscle receives an
insufficient blood supply, causing pain in the chest and often in
the left arm and shoulder. Commonly results when the arteries
supplying the heart muscle (coronaries) are narrowed by atherosclerosis. See *coronary atherosclerosis*.

ANTICOAGULANT   A drug that delays clotting of the blood.
When given in cases of a blood vessel plugged up by a clot, it
tends to prevent new clots from forming, or the existing clots
from enlarging, but does not dissolve an existing clot. Examples
are heparin and coumarin derivatives.

ANXIETY   A feeling of apprehension, the source of which is
unrecognized.

*Some entries have been adapted from *A Handbook of Heart Terms,* Publication No. (NIH) 76–131 of the U.S. Department of Health, Education, and
Welfare.

AORTA   The main trunk artery, which receives blood from the lower left chamber of the heart. It originates from the base of the heart, arches up over the heart like a cane handle, and passes down through the chest and abdomen in front of the spine. It gives off many lesser arteries, which conduct blood to all parts of the body except the lungs.

AORTIC STENOSIS   A narrowing of the valve opening between the lower left chamber of the heart and the aorta. The narrowing may occur at the valve itself or slightly above or below the valve. Aortic stenosis may be the result of scar tissue forming after a rheumatic fever infection, or may have other causes.

AORTIC VALVE   Valve at the junction of the aorta, or large artery, and the lower left chamber of the heart. Formed by three cup-shaped membranes called semilunar valves, it allows the blood to flow from the heart into the artery and prevents a backflow.

ARRHYTHMIA   An abnormal rhythm of the heartbeat.

ARTERIAL BLOOD   Oxygenated blood. The blood is oxygenated in the lungs, passes from the lungs to the left side of the heart via the pulmonary veins, and is then pumped by the heart into the arteries, which carry it to all parts of the body. See *venous blood*.

ARTERIOGRAM (ANGIOGRAM)   X-ray examination of the heart and great blood vessels that follows the course of an opaque fluid that has been injected into the bloodstream.

ARTERIOLES   The smallest arterial vessels (about 1/125 inch in diameter) resulting from repeated branching of the arteries. They conduct blood from the arteries to the capillaries.

ARTERIOSCLEROSIS   Commonly called hardening of the arteries. This is a generic term that includes a variety of conditions that cause the artery walls to become thick and hard and lose elasticity. See *atherosclerosis*.

ARTERY   A blood vessel that carries blood away from the heart to various parts of the body. Arteries usually carry oxygenated blood except for the pulmonary artery, which carries unoxygenated blood from the heart to the lungs for oxygenation. See *vein*.

ATELECTASIS   Inability of the lungs to expand fully.

ATHEROMA   A deposit of fatty (and other) substances in the inner lining of the artery wall, characteristic of atherosclerosis. Plural form of the word is atheromata.

ATHEROSCLEROSIS   A kind of arteriosclerosis in which the inner layer of the artery wall is made thick and irregular by deposits of a fatty substance. These deposits (called atheromata) project above the surface of the inner layer of the artery, and thus decrease the diameter of the internal channel of the vessel. See *arteriosclerosis*.

ATRIOVENTRICULAR VALVES   The two valves, one in each side of the heart, between the upper and lower chamber. The one in the right side of the heart is called the tricuspid valve, and the one in the left side is called the mitral valve.

ATRIUM   One of the two upper chambers of the heart. Also called auricle, although this is now generally used to describe only the very tip of the atrium. The right atrium receives unoxygenated blood from the body. The left atrium receives oxygenated blood from the lungs. Capacity in adults is about 57 cc.

AURICLE   The upper chamber in each side of the heart. "Atrium" is another term commonly used for this chamber.

BACTEREMIA   The presence of bacteria in the bloodstream.

BACTERIAL ENDOCARDITIS   An inflammation of the inner layer of the heart caused by bacteria. The lining of the heart valves is most frequently affected. It is most commonly a complication of an infectious disease, operation, or injury.

BLOOD PRESSURE   The pressure of the blood in the arteries. Blood pressure is generally expressed by two numbers, as 120/80, the first representing the systolic, and the second, the diastolic pressure.

1. Systolic blood pressure. Blood pressure when the heart muscle is contracted (systole).

2. Diastolic blood pressure. Blood pressure when the heart muscle is relaxed between beats (diastole).

BRADYCARDIA   Abnormally slow heart rate. Generally, anything below 60 beats per minute is considered bradycardia.

CAPILLARIES   Extremely narrow tubes forming a network between the arterioles and the veins. The walls are composed of a single layer of cells through which oxygen and nutritive materials pass out to the tissues, and carbon dioxide and waste products are admitted from the tissues into the bloodstream.

CARDIAC   Pertaining to the heart. Sometimes refers to a person who has heart disease.

CARDIAC CYCLE   One total heartbeat, i.e., one complete contraction and relaxation of the heart. In man, this normally occupies about 0.85 second.

CARDIAC OUTPUT   The amount of blood pumped by the heart per minute.

CARDIOVASCULAR   Pertaining to the heart and blood vessels.

CATHETER   A cardiac catheter is a diagnostic device for taking samples of blood or pressure readings within the heart chambers, which might reveal defects in the heart. It is a thin tube of woven plastic or other material to which blood will not adhere, which is inserted in a vein or artery, usually in the arm, and threaded into the heart. The catheter is guided by the physician, who watches its progress by means of x-rays falling on a fluorescent screen. Catheters are also used to enter other tubular organs.

CATHETERIZATION   In cardiology, the process of examining the heart by means of introducing a thin tube (catheter) into a vein or artery and passing it into the heart.

CHOLESTEROL   A fatlike substance found in animal tissue. In blood tests the normal level for Americans is assumed to be between 180 and 230 milligrams per 100 cc. A higher level is often associated with high risk of coronary atherosclerosis.

CIRCULATORY   Pertaining to the heart, blood vessels, and the circulation of the blood.

COAGULATION   Process of changing from a liquid to a thickened or solid state. The formation of a clot.

COARCTATION OF THE AORTA   Literally a pressing together, or a narrowing, of the aorta, the main trunk artery, which conducts blood from the heart to the body. One of several types of congenital heart defects.

COLLATERAL CIRCULATION   Circulation of the blood through nearby smaller vessels when a main vessel has been blocked up.

COMMISSUROTOMY   An operation to widen the opening in a heart valve that has become narrowed by scar tissue. The individual flaps of the valve are cut or spread apart along the natural line of their closure. This operation is often performed in cases of rheumatic heart disease. See *mitral valvulotomy*.

CONGENITAL DEFECT   An abnormality present at birth.

CONGESTIVE HEART FAILURE   When the heart is unable adequately to pump out all the blood that returns to it, there is a backing-up of blood in the veins leading to the heart. A congestion or accumulation of fluid in various parts of the body (lungs, legs, abdomen, etc.) may result from the heart's failure to maintain satisfactory circulation.

CONSTRICTION   Narrowing, as in the phrase "vasoconstriction," which is a narrowing of the internal diameter of the blood vessels, caused by a contraction of the muscular coating of the vessels.

CORONARY ARTERIES   Two arteries arising from the aorta, arching down over the top of the heart, and conducting blood to the heart muscle.

CORONARY ARTERY OCCLUSION   An obstruction (generally a blood clot) in a branch of one of the coronary arteries that hinders the flow of blood to some part of the heart muscle. This part of the heart muscle then dies because of lack of blood supply. Sometimes called a coronary heart attack, or simply a heart attack.

CORONARY ATHEROSCLEROSIS   Commonly called coronary heart disease. An irregular thickening of the inner layer of the walls of the arteries that conduct blood to the heart muscle. The internal channel of these arteries (the coronaries) becomes narrowed and the blood supply to the heart muscle is reduced. See *atherosclerosis*.

CORONARY THROMBOSIS   Formation of a clot in one of the arteries that conduct blood to the heart muscle.

DEFIBRILLATOR   Any agent or measure, such as an electric shock, that stops an uncoordinated contraction of the heart and restores a normal heartbeat.

DIASTOLE   In each heartbeat, the period of the relaxation of the heart. Auricular diastole is the period of relaxation of the atria, or upper heart chambers. Ventricular diastole is the period of relaxation of the ventricles, or lower heart chambers.

DIGITALIS   A drug prepared from leaves of the foxglove plant that strengthens the contraction of the heart muscle, slows the rate of contraction of the heart, and by improving the efficiency of the heart may promote the elimination of fluid from body tissues.

DIURETIC   A medicine that promotes the excretion of urine. Several types of drugs may be used, such as mercurials, chlorothiazide, xanthine, and benzothiadiazine derivatives.

DUCTUS ARTERIOSUS   A small opening in the heart of the fetus between the artery leaving the left side of the heart (aorta) and the artery leaving the right side of the heart (pulmonary artery). Normally this duct closes soon after birth. If it does not close, the condition is known as patent or open ductus arteriosus. See *patent ductus arteriosus*.

DYSPNEA   Difficult or labored breathing.

EDEMA   Swelling due to abnormally large amounts of fluid in the tissues of the body.

ELECTROCARDIOGRAM   Often referred to as EKG or ECG. A graphic record of the electric currents produced by the heart.

ELECTROCARDIOGRAPH   An instrument that records electric currents produced by the heart.

EMBOLISM   The blocking of a blood vessel by a clot or other substance carried in the bloodstream.

EMBOLUS   A blood clot (or other substance such as air, fat, tumor) inside a blood vessel that is carried in the bloodstream to a smaller vessel where it becomes an obstruction to circulation. See *thrombus*.

FIBRILLATION   Uncoordinated contractions of the heart occurring when the individual muscle fibers take up independent irregular contractions.

HEART BLOCK   Interference with the conduction of the electrical impulses of the heart, which can be either partial or complete.

This can result in dissociation of the rhythms of the upper and lower heart chambers.

HEART-LUNG MACHINE   A machine through which the blood-stream is diverted for pumping and oxygenation while the heart is opened for surgery.

HEMOGLOBIN   The oxygen-carrying red pigment of the red blood corpuscles. When it has absorbed oxygen in the lungs, it is bright red and called oxy-hemoglobin. After it has given up its oxygen load in the tissues, it is purple in color, and is called reduced hemoglobin.

HEMORRHAGE   Loss of blood from a blood vessel. In external hemorrhage blood escapes from the body. In internal hemor-rhage blood passes into tissues surrounding the ruptured blood vessel.

HYPERCHOLESTEROLEMIA   An excess of a fatty substance called cholesterol in the blood. Sometimes called hypercholesteremia or hypercholesterinemia. See *cholesterol.*

HYPERTENSION   Commonly called high blood pressure. An un-stable or persistent elevation of blood pressure above the normal range, which may eventually lead to increased heart size and kidney damage.

INCOMPETENT VALVE   Any valve that does not close tight and leaks blood back in the wrong direction. Also called valvular insufficiency.

INFARCT   An area of a tissue that is damaged or dies as a result of not receiving a sufficient blood supply. Frequently used in the phrase "myocardial infarct," referring to an area of the heart muscle damaged or killed by an insufficient flow of blood through the coronary arteries that normally supply it.

INSUFFICIENCY   Incompetency. In the term "valvular insufficiency," an improper closing of the valves that admits a backflow of blood in the wrong direction. In the term "myocardial insufficiency," inability of the heart muscle to do a normal pumping job.

INTIMA   The innermost layer of a blood vessel.

ISCHEMIA   A local, usually temporary, deficiency of blood in some part of the body, often caused by a constriction of or an obstruction in the blood vessel supplying that part.

MITRAL INSUFFICIENCY   An improper closing of the mitral valve between the upper and lower chambers in the left side of the heart, which admits a backflow of blood. Sometimes the result of scar tissue forming after a rheumatic fever infection.

MITRAL STENOSIS   A narrowing of the valve (called the bicuspid or mitral valve) opening between the upper and the lower chambers in the left side of the heart. Sometimes the result of scar tissue forming after a rheumatic fever infection.

MITRAL VALVE   Sometimes called bicuspid valve. A valve of two cusps or triangular segments, located between the upper and lower chambers in the left side of the heart.

MITRAL VALVULOTOMY   An operation to widen the opening in the valve between the upper and lower chambers in the left side of the heart (mitral valve). Usually performed when the valve opening is so narrowed as to obstruct blood flow, which sometimes happens as a result of rheumatic fever.

MONOUNSATURATED FAT   A fat so constituted chemically that it is capable of absorbing additional hydrogen but not as much hydrogen as a polyunsaturated fat. These fats in the diet have little effect on the amount of cholesterol in the blood. One example is olive oil. See *polyunsaturated fat.*

MURMUR   An abnormal heart sound, similar to that of fluid passing an obstruction, heard between the normal "lub-dub" heart sounds.

MYOCARDIAL INFARCTION   The damaging or death of an area of the heart muscle (myocardium) resulting from a reduction in the blood supply reaching that area.

MYOCARDIUM   The muscular wall of the heart. The thickest of the three layers of the heart wall, it lies between the inner layer (endocardium) and the outer layer (epicardium).

NITROGLYCERIN   A drug (one of the nitrates) that relaxes the muscles in the blood vessels. Often used to relieve attacks of angina and spasm of coronary arteries. It is one of the vasodilators.

OPEN HEART SURGERY   Surgery performed on the heart while the bloodstream is diverted through a heart-lung machine. This machine pumps and oxygenates the blood in lieu of the action of the heart and lungs during the operation.

PACEMAKER   A small mass of specialized cells in the right upper chamber of the heart that gives rise to the electrical impulses that initiate contractions of the heart. Also called sinoatrial node or SA node of Keith-Flack. The term "pacemaker," or more exactly, "electric cardiac pacemaker," or "electrical pacemaker," is applied to an electrical device that can substitute for a defective natural pacemaker and control the beating of the heart by a series of rhythmic electrical discharges. If the electrodes that deliver the discharges to the heart are placed on the outside of the chest, it is called an external pacemaker. If the electrodes are placed within the chest wall, it is called an internal pacemaker.

PALPITATION   A fluttering of the heart or abnormal rate or rhythm of the heart experienced by the person himself.

PATENT DUCTUS ARTERIOSUS   A congenital heart defect in which a small duct between the artery leaving the left side of the heart (aorta) and the artery leaving the right side of the heart (pulmonary artery), which normally closes soon after birth, remains open. As a result of this duct's failure to close, blood from both sides of the heart is pumped into the pulmonary artery and into the lungs. This defect is sometimes called simply "patent ductus." Patent means open.

PERCUSSION   Tapping the body as an aid in diagnosing the condition of parts beneath by the sound obtained, much as one taps on a barrel to detect its fullness.

PERICARDITIS   Inflammation of the thin membrane sac (pericardium) that surrounds the heart.

PERICARDIUM   A thin membrane sac that surrounds the heart and roots of the great vessels.

PHLEBITIS   Inflammation of a vein, often in the leg. Sometimes a blood clot is formed in the inflamed vein.

POLYUNSATURATED FAT   A fat so constituted chemically that it is capable of absorbing additional hydrogen. These fats are usually liquid oils of vegetable origin, such as corn oil or safflower oil. A diet with a high polyunsaturated fat content tends to lower the amount of cholesterol in the blood. These fats are sometimes substituted for saturated fat in a diet in an effort to lessen the hazard of fatty deposits in the blood vessels. See *monounsaturated fat.*

PULMONARY ARTERY   The large artery that conveys unoxygenated (venous) blood from the lower right chamber of the heart to the lungs. This is the only artery in the body that carries unoxygenated blood, all others carrying oxygenated blood to the body.

PULMONARY VALVE   Valve formed by three cup-shaped membranes at the junction of the pulmonary artery and the right lower chamber of the heart (right ventricle). When the right lower chamber contracts, the pulmonary valve opens and the blood is forced into the artery leading to the lungs. When the chamber relaxes, the valve is closed and prevents backflow of the blood.

PULMONARY VEINS   Four veins (two from each lung) that conduct oxygenated blood from the lungs into the left upper chamber of the heart (left atrium).

PULSE   The expansion and contraction of an artery, which may be felt with the finger.

RHEUMATIC FEVER   A disease, usually occurring in childhood, that may follow a few weeks after a streptococcal infection. It is sometimes characterized by one or more of the following: fever, sore, swollen joints, a skin rash, occasionally involuntary twitching of the muscles (called chorea or St. Vitus' Dance), and small nodes under the skin. In some cases the infection affects the heart and may result in scarring the valves, weakening the heart muscle, or damaging the sac enclosing the heart. See *rheumatic heart disease.*

RHEUMATIC HEART DISEASE   The damage done to the heart, particularly the heart valves, by one or more attacks of rheumatic fever. The valves are sometimes scarred so they do not open and close normally. See *rheumatic fever.*

SAPHENOUS VEIN   Either of two large, superficial veins of the foot, leg, and thigh, one on the inner side and the other on the outer and posterior sides.

SATURATED FAT   A fat so constituted chemically that it is not capable of absorbing any more hydrogen. These are usually the solid fats of animal origin, such as the fats in milk, butter, meat,

203 | GLOSSARY OF MEDICAL TERMS

etc. A diet high in saturated fats tends to increase the amount of cholesterol in the blood. Sometimes these fats are restricted in the diet in an effort to lessen the hazard of fatty deposits in the blood vessels.

SEPTUM   The muscular wall dividing the left and right chambers of the heart.

STENOSIS   A narrowing or stricture of an opening. Mitral stenosis, aortic stenosis, etc., means that the valve indicated has become narrowed so that it does not function normally.

TACHYCARDIA   Abnormally fast heart rate. Generally, anything over 100 beats per minute is considered a tachycardia.

THROMBOSIS   The formation or presence of a blood clot (thrombus) inside a blood vessel or cavity of the heart.

THROMBUS   A blood clot that forms inside a blood vessel or cavity of the heart. See *embolus.*

TRICUSPID VALVE   A valve consisting of three cusps or triangular segments, located between the upper and lower chambers of the right side of the heart.

VALVULAR INSUFFICIENCY   Valves that close improperly and admit a backflow of blood. See *incompetent valve.*

VASODILATOR   Vasodilator nerves are certain nerve fibers of the involuntary nervous system that cause the muscles of the arterioles to relax, thus enlarging the arteriole passage, reducing resistance to the flow of blood, and lowering blood pressure.

   Vasodilator agents are chemical compounds that cause a relaxation of the muscles of the arterioles. Examples of this type of drug are nitroglycerin, nitrates, thiocyanate, and many others.

VEIN   Any one of a series of vessels of the vascular system that carries blood from various parts of the body back to the heart.

All veins in the body conduct unoxygenated blood except the pulmonary veins, which conduct freshly oxygenated blood from the lungs back to the heart.

VENA CAVA   The superior vena cava is a large vein conducting blood from the upper part of the body to the right atrium. The inferior vena cava brings blood from the lower part of the body into the right atrium.

VENOUS BLOOD   Unoxygenated blood. The blood, with hemoglobin in the reduced state, is carried by the veins from all parts of the body back to the heart.

VENTRICLE   One of the two lower chambers of the heart. The left ventricle pumps oxygenated blood through arteries to the body. The right ventricle pumps unoxygenated blood through the pulmonary artery to the lungs. Capacity is about 85 cc.

Index

About the Author

INA L. YALOF was born in Chicago and grew up in Miami Beach. While she was still in college she received two fellowships for sociological research in medicine in 1973 and 1974. In 1975 she assumed her present position as a medical sociologist and a member of the open heart surgery team at Newark Beth Israel Medical Center. She lives in New Jersey with her husband and three children.